Breaking into Grant writing:
Tips and Strategies

By

Queen Israel

Disclaimer

The information provided in this book, "Breaking Into Grant Writing: Strategies and Tips" is for educational purposes only. While the author has made every effort to ensure the accuracy and completeness of the information provided, the author makes no guarantee that the information is current or suitable for any particular purpose. The author is not responsible for any errors or omissions in the information provided, or for any damages or losses that may result from the use of the information.

The information provided in this book is not intended to be legal or professional advice, and readers should consult with a qualified professional before making any decisions based on the information provided in this book. The author is not liable for any damages or losses that may result from any errors or omissions in the information provided in this book, or from any actions taken based on the information provided.

The mention of any product, service, or organization in this book does not imply endorsement by the author, and the author is not responsible for any damages or losses that may result from the use of any product, service, or organization mentioned in this book.

The author reserves the right to make changes to the information provided in this book at any time and without notice. Readers are responsible for keeping up to date with any changes or updates to the information provided in this book.

By using the information provided in this book, readers acknowledge that they have read and understood this disclaimer and agree to its terms.

Dedication:

This book is dedicated to all grant writers and passionate nonprofits who work tirelessly to make our world a better place. Your unwavering commitment to creating positive change is truly inspiring, and this book is a tribute to your dedication and hard work.

May the insights and strategies shared in this book serve as a valuable resource in your efforts to secure the funding needed to advance your mission and make a lasting impact. Thank you for all that you do.

Acknowledgement

I would like to express my deepest gratitude to everyone who helped make this book a reality.

First and foremost, I would like to thank God Almighty for His Infinite wisdom.

Secondly, my family for their unwavering support and encouragement throughout this journey. To my loving son, Elvis Nweke, and my husband, Samuel Nweke, thank you for understanding the long hours and countless weekends spent working on this book. Your love and support have been invaluable to me.

I am also grateful to the many colleagues and professionals in the grant writing industry who generously shared their insights and expertise. Your guidance and feedback have been instrumental in shaping the content of this book.

I would also like to extend my appreciation to the team at the publishing company for their assistance and support throughout the publishing process.

Finally, I want to express my sincere gratitude to the readers of this book. I hope that the knowledge and strategies shared in these pages will empower you to achieve your grant writing goals and make a difference in the world.

Thank you all for your contributions and support.

Sincerely,

Queen

Preface

Welcome to Breaking into Grant Writing! This book is a comprehensive guide for individuals who aspire to build a career in grant writing, as well as seasoned professionals looking to enhance their skills and knowledge.

Throughout this book, we will cover a wide range of topics, from the basics of grant writing to advanced strategies for building a successful career in this field. You will learn how to identify funding opportunities, craft compelling grant proposals, develop effective data and evaluation plans, collaborate with partners, and more.

As you read through these pages, you will find a wealth of practical advice and real-world examples to help you master the craft of grant writing. You will also gain insight into the various challenges and obstacles that you may encounter along the way, and learn strategies for overcoming them.

Grant writing is a dynamic and constantly evolving field, and staying up-to-date with the latest trends and best practices is critical for success. That is why we have included a section on professional development, to help you continue to grow and learn throughout your career.

Whether you are just starting out or are a seasoned professional, Breaking into Grant Writing is an essential resource for anyone looking to build a successful career in this field. We hope that you find this book to be informative, engaging, and inspiring, and that it helps you achieve your goals in grant writing.

Best of luck on your journey!

Table of Contents

Part 1

Introduction

Welcome to "Breaking into Grant Writing: Tips and Strategies." This book is designed to provide you with a comprehensive introduction to the world of grant writing and equip you with the essential skills and knowledge you need to get started in this field.

But first, what exactly is grant writing?

In essence, grant writing involves creating proposals to secure funding from foundations, corporations, and government agencies for a wide range of projects, programs, and initiatives.

Grant writers work with non-profit organizations, schools, universities, government agencies, and other institutions to help them obtain the financial resources they need to carry out their missions and serve their communities.

Why does grant writing matter?

Simply put, grant funding can make a huge difference in the success of an organization or project. Grants can provide critical resources for research, innovation, education, and community development, helping to address important social and economic challenges.

In today's increasingly competitive funding environment, strong grant writing skills are more important than ever to help organizations secure the resources they need to make a positive impact.

So, what does it take to become a successful grant writer?

It's important to understand that grant writing requires a unique set of skills and knowledge. You need to be able to research and identify funding opportunities that match your organization's mission and goals.

You also need to be able to create compelling proposals that clearly communicate your organization's strengths, goals, and outcomes. This involves not only strong writing skills but also an ability to understand and apply research and evaluation techniques.

In addition to these technical skills, successful grant writers need to possess a few key traits. You need to be self-motivated, able to work independently and meet deadlines. You also need to be detail-oriented, able to manage multiple projects and budgets, and comfortable working with diverse groups of people.

To develop these skills and traits, it's important to have a strong foundation in the basics of grant writing. This includes a comprehensive understanding of the grant writing process, from researching funding opportunities to submitting proposals and managing grants.

It also includes knowledge of the legal and ethical considerations of grant writing, such as ensuring compliance with funder requirements and managing conflicts of interest.

Education and training are also critical to developing the skills you need to succeed in grant writing. This might include pursuing a degree or certification in grant writing or a related field, attending workshops and conferences, and seeking out mentors and networking opportunities in the grant writing community.

At the end of the day, grant writing is a complex and rewarding field that requires a unique combination of skills, knowledge, and personal traits. With the right guidance and support, anyone can develop the expertise they need to succeed in grant writing and make a positive impact in their community.

Throughout this book, we'll provide you with the tools, tips, and strategies you need to do just that.

What Is Grant Writing?

Grant writing is the art of crafting proposals to secure funding from a variety of sources, including government agencies, corporations, and foundations. Grants are typically awarded to support a wide range of programs, projects, and initiatives, ranging from scientific research to community development.

As a grant writer, your job is to research available funding opportunities and identify the grants that match your organization's mission and goals. This can involve reviewing grant databases and publications, attending workshops and webinars, and networking with other grant writers and funding organizations.

Once you've identified a potential funding source, you'll need to create a compelling proposal that clearly communicates your organization's strengths, goals, and outcomes. This involves not only strong writing skills but also an ability to understand and apply research and evaluation techniques.

At the heart of any successful grant proposal is a clear and concise statement of need. This should describe the problem or issue that your organization seeks to address and explain why it is important to the community. You'll also need to provide a detailed plan of action that outlines the steps your organization will take to address the problem, as well as a budget that shows how the grant funding will be used.

In addition to these core components, successful grant proposals often include other elements such as a well-crafted cover letter, an executive summary that highlights the key points of the proposal, and a strong data and evaluation plan that demonstrates the impact of the project.

Grant writing is not just about writing proposals, however. It also involves building relationships with funders, networking with other grant writers, and managing grants once they've been awarded. This can include preparing progress reports, managing budgets, and ensuring compliance with funder requirements.

Successful grant writing requires a combination of technical skills, personal traits, and knowledge. You need to be a strong writer, able to convey complex ideas clearly and concisely. You also need to be detail-oriented, able to manage multiple projects and deadlines, and comfortable working with diverse groups of people.

And, of course, you need to have a deep understanding of the grant writing process and the legal and ethical considerations involved.

Despite the challenges of grant writing, it can be an extremely rewarding and impactful career. By securing funding for important programs and projects, grant writers can help organizations make a real difference in their communities. And with the right training, education, and support, anyone can develop the skills and expertise needed

to become a successful grant writer.

Why Grant Writing Matters?

Grant writing is a critical component of the nonprofit sector and plays a vital role in securing funding for organizations that are committed to making a difference in their communities.

The importance of grant writing cannot be overstated, as it allows organizations to pursue projects and initiatives that they would not otherwise have the resources to undertake.

At its core, grant writing is all about communicating a compelling story that resonates with potential funders. Successful grant proposals are built on strong narratives that outline the impact that an organization hopes to achieve and demonstrate why the proposed project is important and worth funding.

Grants are essential to nonprofit organizations because they provide the necessary resources to carry out projects and initiatives that are aligned with the organization's mission and goals.

Many nonprofits are working to address some of the most pressing social issues of our time, from hunger and homelessness to environmental degradation and inequality. However, these organizations are often stretched thin and lack the resources to fully realize their goals.

Grants provide the financial support needed to turn ambitious goals into tangible outcomes. For example, a grant could provide funding to help a local food bank purchase a refrigerated truck to transport fresh produce to underserved communities. Or it could help a community organization launch a mentorship program for at-risk youth.

These are just a few examples of how grants can make a real difference in people's lives.

In addition to providing funding, grants also offer a range of benefits to nonprofits. For one, they provide an opportunity for organizations to build relationships with funders and expand their networks. This can lead to future funding opportunities and partnerships that can help the organization grow and expand its impact.

Grants also help organizations to better understand and measure the impact of their work. Many grants require organizations to develop detailed plans for measuring outcomes and evaluating the success of their projects. This can help organizations to refine their programs and initiatives, ensuring that they are delivering the most impact for the resources invested.

For individuals interested in pursuing a career in the nonprofit sector, grant writing can be an incredibly rewarding and fulfilling profession. Grant writers have the opportunity to work with a variety of organizations and causes, helping to make a real difference in their communities. The skills and expertise gained through grant writing can also be highly transferable, opening up a range of career opportunities within the nonprofit sector.

However, grant writing is not without its challenges. Securing grants is highly competitive, and it requires a great deal of work to develop a successful proposal.

Additionally, the grant landscape is constantly evolving, with new funding opportunities emerging all the time. Staying up-to-date with the latest trends and best practices is essential for any grant writer looking to remain competitive in the field.

In conclusion, grant writing matters because it allows nonprofits to secure the funding they need to carry out important projects and initiatives that are aligned with their missions and goals. Grants provide a range of benefits to nonprofits, including funding, networking opportunities, and support for measuring and evaluating the impact of their work. For individuals interested in a career in the nonprofit sector, grant writing can be an incredibly rewarding and impactful profession that allows them to make a real difference in the world.

Part 2
Getting Started in Grant writing

Getting started in grant writing can be a daunting task, but with the right approach and some hard work, anyone can break into this exciting and rewarding field.

This section will provide an overview of the key steps you need to take to get started in grant writing, including how to build your skills, find opportunities, and prepare successful proposals.

1. Develop Your Grant Writing Skills

To succeed as a grant writer, you will need to have a strong set of skills that allow you to craft compelling proposals that resonate with funders. Some of the key skills you will need to develop include:

- **Research**: Grant writers need to be able to conduct thorough research to identify funding opportunities that are a good fit for their organization's goals and mission.
- **Writing**: Strong writing skills are essential for creating proposals that are clear, concise, and persuasive. It is important to be able to convey complex information in a way that is easy to understand for funders.
- **Communication**: In addition to writing, grant writers need to be skilled communicators who can collaborate effectively with other members of their organization and build relationships with funders.
- **Project Management**: Grant writing involves coordinating various stakeholders and managing timelines and budgets to ensure that proposals are completed on time and within budget.

To build these skills, there are a number of resources available to aspiring grant writers. These include online courses, webinars, and workshops that cover various aspects of grant writing, as well as mentorship programs and networking opportunities.

2. Identify Funding Opportunities

Once you have developed your grant writing skills, the next step is to identify funding opportunities that are a good fit for your organization. There are many resources available to help you find grants, including:

- **Online databases**: There are a number of online databases that list current grant opportunities, including Grant Watch, Foundation Center, and Grant Station.
- **Government agencies**: Federal, state, and local government agencies offer a range of grant opportunities in various fields, such as health, education, and the environment.
- **Private foundations**: Private foundations offer funding for a range of causes, including education, the arts, and social justice.
- **Corporate giving programs**: Many corporations have giving programs that support various causes, such as employee volunteerism and community development.

When identifying funding opportunities, it is important to ensure that the grants you are applying for are aligned with your organization's mission and goals.

It is also important to carefully review the application guidelines and eligibility requirements to ensure that your organization meets the necessary criteria.

3. Prepare Your Grant Proposal

Once you have identified a funding opportunity that is a good fit for your organization, the next step is to prepare your grant proposal. This is where your grant writing skills will come into play.

To create a successful proposal, you will need to:

- **Understand the funder's priorities**: Before starting your proposal, take the time to understand the funder's priorities and interests. This will help you tailor your proposal to their specific needs and goals.
- **Develop a compelling narrative**: Your proposal should tell a clear and compelling story that outlines the problem you are trying to solve, your approach to solving it, and the impact you hope to achieve.
- **Use data and evidence**: It is important to use data and evidence to support your proposal and demonstrate the effectiveness of your approach.
- **Follow the application guidelines**: Make sure to carefully follow the application guidelines and requirements to ensure that your proposal is considered.
- **Edit and revise**: Once you have completed your proposal, make sure to edit and revise it to ensure that it is clear, concise, and persuasive.
4. **Submit Your Proposal:** After you have prepared your grant proposal, the final step is to submit it to the funder. It is important to carefully review the submission guidelines and ensure that you submit your proposal on time and in the correct format.

In addition, it is a good idea to follow up with the funder after submitting your proposal to confirm receipt and to thank them for their consideration.

5. Continue Building Your Skills and Experience

Even if your first grant proposal is not successful, it is important to continue building your skills and experience in grant writing. This can include seeking feedback on your proposals, attending workshops and webinars to continue learning about the field, and networking with other grant writers and funders.

Over time, with persistence and hard work, you can build a successful career in grant writing and help secure critical funding for the organizations and causes you care about.

6. Consider Working with a Grant Writer or Consultant

If you are new to grant writing or feel overwhelmed by the process, you may want to consider working with a grant writer or consultant. These professionals have expertise in writing and submitting successful grant proposals and can help guide you through the process.

Working with a grant writer or consultant can also help you to identify new funding opportunities and build relationships with funders.

Additionally, they can provide feedback on your proposals and help you to improve your grant writing skills over time.

7. Be Persistent and Patient

Breaking into grant writing takes time, effort, and persistence. Not every proposal will be successful, and it may take time to build relationships with funders and find the right opportunities for your organization.

However, it is important to remain patient and persistent, continuing to build your skills and experience over time.

Remember that each proposal is an opportunity to learn and grow as a grant writer, and with each submission, you are building your network of contacts and potential funders.

Getting started in grant writing requires a combination of skills, resources, and persistence. By building your skills, identifying funding opportunities, preparing compelling proposals, and submitting them to funders, you can begin to break into this rewarding and meaningful field. With patience, persistence, and hard work, you can help secure the critical funding needed to support important causes and make a positive impact in the world.

Essential Skills for Grant Writers

Grant writing is a specialized field that requires a unique set of skills and knowledge to be successful. Whether you are new to grant writing or an experienced professional, it is essential to have a strong understanding of the skills and competencies required to succeed in this field.

Here are some of the essential skills for grant writers:

1. **Strong Writing Skills**

The ability to write clear, concise, and compelling proposals is essential for grant writers. You need to be able to communicate your organization's mission and goals effectively, and articulate how the proposed project will meet the needs of the community or population being served.

You should also be able to write persuasively and convincingly, highlighting the impact and potential outcomes of the project. This requires strong research skills, an ability to synthesize complex information, and a knack for storytelling.

2. Research Skills

A significant part of grant writing involves identifying funding opportunities and conducting research to gather information about potential funders. You need to be able to identify potential funders, understand their funding priorities and guidelines, and tailor your proposals to meet their specific requirements.

Strong research skills also help you to develop evidence-based proposals that are supported by data and research. You should be able to identify relevant statistics and other evidence to support your proposal, as well as assess the feasibility of your proposed project.

3. Project Management Skills

Successful grant writers need to be able to manage multiple projects simultaneously and meet strict deadlines. You should be able to develop detailed project plans and budgets, and have a clear understanding of the resources required to complete the project.

You should also have strong organizational skills, as well as an ability to prioritize tasks and manage your time effectively. This requires strong attention to detail and an ability to work independently and with a team.

4. Communication and Interpersonal Skills

Grant writing is a collaborative process that involves working with team members, stakeholders, and funders. You should have strong communication and interpersonal skills to build relationships with funders, respond to questions and requests, and maintain positive relationships with stakeholders.

You should also be able to work collaboratively with other team members, such as program staff and development staff, to ensure that the project is aligned with the organization's mission and goals.

5. Financial Management Skills

Grant writers need to have a basic understanding of financial management, including how to develop and manage budgets, track expenses, and analyze financial reports. You should be able to identify and mitigate financial risks, as well as ensure that the proposed project is financially feasible and sustainable.

6. Adaptability and Flexibility

Grant writing is a fast-paced and dynamic field that requires adaptability and flexibility. You should be able to adapt to changing funding priorities and guidelines, as well as changes in the project scope or timeline.

You should also be able to think creatively and develop innovative solutions to challenges and obstacles that arise during the grant writing process.

In Summary, successful grant writers need a combination of strong writing, research, project management, communication, financial management, and adaptability skills. By developing and honing these essential competencies, you can become a successful grant writer and help secure critical funding for important causes and organizations.

Education and Training for Grant Writers

While there is no single educational path for becoming a grant writer, there are a variety of education and training options that can help you develop the skills and knowledge required for success in this field.

Here are some of the education and training options available for aspiring grant writers:

1. **Bachelor's or Master's Degree**

   A bachelor's or master's degree in a related field such as nonprofit management, public policy, social work, or business can provide a strong foundation in the skills required for grant writing. These programs can provide training in grant research, proposal development, financial management, and project management.

   Some programs may also offer internships or other hands-on opportunities to gain experience in the field.

2. **Professional Development Programs**

   Many organizations offer professional development programs or workshops that focus specifically on grant writing. These programs may provide training in specific areas such as research, writing, budgeting, or project management. Some programs may also offer opportunities to network with other grant writers and connect with potential funders.

3. Certifications

There are a variety of certification programs available for grant writers. These programs may focus on a specific area of grant writing such as proposal development, grant research, or financial management. Certifications can provide validation of your skills and knowledge and demonstrate your commitment to professional development.

4. On-the-Job Training

Many grant writers learn on the job, gaining experience through their work with nonprofit organizations, government agencies, or other grant-funded projects. This on-the-job training can provide hands-on experience in all aspects of the grant writing process, from identifying funding opportunities to managing projects and reporting on outcomes.

5. Volunteer Experience

Volunteering with a nonprofit organization can provide valuable experience in grant writing and related areas such as fundraising, marketing, and community outreach. Volunteer opportunities may involve grant research, proposal development, or grant reporting, and can help you develop your skills and build your network in the nonprofit sector.

Regardless of the education or training path you choose, it's important to continue learning and staying up-to-date with the latest trends and best practices in grant writing. This may involve attending conferences, webinars, or workshops, reading industry publications, or participating in professional organizations.

In addition to formal education and training, there are also a variety of personal attributes that can contribute to success in grant writing.

These include:

1. **Curiosity and a Passion for Learning**

Successful grant writers are curious and have a passion for learning. They stay up-to-date on the latest trends and best practices in the field, and are always seeking new opportunities to improve their skills and knowledge.

2. **Creativity and Innovation**

Grant writing often requires thinking creatively and developing innovative solutions to complex problems. Successful grant writers are able to approach problems from different angles and develop proposals that are both feasible and impactful.

3. **Attention to Detail**

The grant writing process requires attention to detail, from developing budgets to ensuring compliance with funder guidelines. Successful grant writers are able to keep track of multiple details and maintain accuracy throughout the proposal development process.

4. **Persistence and Resilience**

Grant writing can be a challenging and competitive field, with a high rate of rejection for proposals. Successful grant writers are persistent and resilient, continuing to develop proposals and seek funding even in the face of rejection or setbacks.

Building a Foundation for Success

Building a strong foundation is key to success in any endeavor, and grant writing is no exception.

In this section, we will explore some of the key elements that are essential for building a strong foundation for success in grant writing.

1. **Define your Purpose and Goals**

   Before embarking on any grant writing project, it's important to define your purpose and goals. What are you trying to achieve through this project? What are the specific outcomes you hope to see?

   Having a clear understanding of your purpose and goals will help guide your research and proposal development, and ensure that you are targeting the right funders and opportunities.

2. **Identify your Target Audience**

   One of the keys to successful grant writing is understanding your target audience. Who are the funders you are seeking to engage with? What are their priorities and values? What are the specific requirements and guidelines they have for proposals? Understanding your target audience will help you develop proposals that are both compelling and responsive to the needs and priorities of funders.

3. Develop a Strong Concept

The concept is the core idea that underpins your grant proposal. A strong concept is one that is well-defined, feasible, and aligned with the priorities and values of funders. To develop a strong concept, it's important to conduct thorough research into the issue or problem you are seeking to address, and to consider a range of potential solutions and approaches.

4. Conduct Thorough Research

Research is an essential component of grant writing, as it helps to inform your proposal development and ensure that your concept is well-supported and responsive to the needs and priorities of funders.

Research may include gathering data and statistics, conducting needs assessments and stakeholder consultations, and reviewing existing research and best practices.

5. Develop a Realistic Budget

A realistic budget is a critical component of any grant proposal, as it demonstrates to funders that you have thought through the costs and resources required to implement your project.

To develop a realistic budget, it's important to consider all of the costs associated with your project, including personnel, equipment, supplies, and indirect costs. It's also important to be transparent and accurate in your budget development, and to ensure that your budget aligns with the requirements and guidelines of funders.

6. Build Strong Partnerships

Building strong partnerships is an essential component of successful grant writing. Collaborating with other organizations and stakeholders can help to strengthen your proposal and increase its chances of success. Strong partnerships may include organizations with complementary missions or expertise, community groups, or academic institutions.

7. Develop a Strong Narrative

The narrative is the heart of your grant proposal, and is where you tell the story of your project and demonstrate its impact and feasibility. A strong narrative is one that is compelling, clear, and well-supported by evidence and data.

To develop a strong narrative, it's important to focus on the key messages and themes of your proposal, and to use language and examples that are accessible and engaging to your target audience.

8. Ensure Compliance

It's important to ensure that your grant proposal is in compliance with all relevant laws, regulations, and guidelines. This includes ensuring that your proposal meets the eligibility requirements of funders, and that it aligns with any specific guidelines or requirements they may have.

It's also important to ensure that your proposal adheres to any ethical or legal standards, and that you have obtained

all necessary approvals or permissions.

9. Stay Organized

Grant writing can be a complex and time-consuming process, and it's important to stay organized to ensure that you are meeting all deadlines and requirements. This may involve creating a project management plan, using tools like spreadsheets or project management software to track your progress, and maintaining a centralized location for all documents and resources related to your proposal.

10. Seek Feedback

Getting feedback from peers, mentors, or other professionals in the field is an essential component of building a strong foundation for success in grant writing.

Feedback can help you identify areas where your proposal could be strengthened or improved, and can also provide valuable insight into the priorities and values of funders. Seeking feedback can also help you build relationships with other professionals in the field, and can provide opportunities for professional growth and development.

11. Develop a Professional Network

Developing a professional network is another key element of building a strong foundation for success in grant writing. This may involve attending conferences, workshops, or other professional development opportunities, as well as seeking out mentorship or guidance from more experienced grant writers or professionals in the field.

Building a strong professional network can provide opportunities for learning, growth, and collaboration, and can also help you stay up-to-date with emerging trends and best practices in grant writing.

12. Be Persistent

Finally, persistence is an essential component of building a strong foundation for success in grant writing. Grant writing can be a competitive and challenging field, and it's important to remain persistent and resilient in the face of setbacks or challenges.

This may involve continuing to research new funding opportunities, seeking feedback and guidance from others, and remaining committed to your goals and purpose.

Part 3
The Grant Writing Process

The grant writing process is a complex and multifaceted undertaking that requires a clear understanding of the funder's requirements and priorities, as well as a strong grasp of the elements that make up a compelling and competitive proposal.

In this section, we'll take a closer look at the key steps involved in the grant writing process, and provide practical tips and strategies for success.

Step 1: Review the Funding Opportunity

The first step in the grant writing process is to review the funding opportunity to determine if it's a good fit for your organization or project.

This may involve conducting a thorough review of the funder's priorities, requirements, and guidelines, as well as researching past grantees and projects to gain a better understanding of the funder's priorities and values.

It's important to pay close attention to the funding opportunity's purpose and goals, as well as the eligibility criteria and application requirements.

This information will help guide your approach to developing a strong proposal, and will also help you determine if your project is a good fit for the funder's priorities and values.

Step 2: Develop a Strong Concept

Once you've reviewed the funding opportunity and determined that it's a good fit for your organization or project, the next step is to develop a strong concept for your proposal.

This may involve conducting further research to identify the key issues and challenges that your project addresses, as well as developing a clear and compelling narrative that outlines the goals and objectives of your project.

It's important to focus on the funder's priorities and values when developing your concept, and to clearly articulate how your project aligns with these priorities. This will help to demonstrate the relevance and importance of your project, and will also increase your chances of success in securing funding.

Step 3: Write the Proposal

With a strong concept in hand, the next step is to write the proposal. This may involve following a specific format or structure outlined in the funding opportunity guidelines, and may also involve developing specific sections or components, such as a project description, budget, or timeline.

It's important to pay close attention to the details when writing your proposal, and to ensure that all requirements and guidelines are met.

This may involve revising and editing your proposal multiple times to ensure that it's clear, concise, and compelling, and that it aligns with the funder's priorities and values.

Step 4: Seek Feedback

Once you've written your proposal, it's important to seek feedback from peers, mentors, or other professionals in the field. This feedback can help you identify areas where your proposal could be strengthened or improved, and can also provide valuable insight into the priorities and values of funders.

It's important to seek feedback from individuals with experience in grant writing or in the specific field or issue area that your project addresses. This feedback can help you refine your proposal and increase your chances of success in securing funding.

Step 5: Submit the Proposal

The final step in the grant writing process is to submit your proposal to the funder. This may involve following specific submission guidelines and requirements, and may also involve submitting supporting materials or documentation.

It's important to pay close attention to the submission deadline and to ensure that all requirements are met in a timely and complete manner.

This will help to increase your chances of success in securing funding and will also demonstrate your professionalism and attention to detail.

Here are a few additional tips and strategies to help you succeed in the grant writing process:

1. **Build Strong Relationships**

Building strong relationships with funders and other professionals in the field can be a key factor in the success of your grant proposal. This may involve attending conferences, networking events, or other professional gatherings, as well as engaging with funders through social media or other online platforms.

By building strong relationships with funders and other professionals, you can gain valuable insights into their priorities and values, as well as access to additional funding opportunities and resources.

2. Focus on Outcomes and Impact

When developing your grant proposal, it's important to focus on the outcomes and impact of your project.

This may involve identifying specific metrics or indicators that will be used to measure success, as well as outlining the potential impact of your project on the community or field.

By focusing on outcomes and impact, you can demonstrate the relevance and importance of your project, and increase your chances of success in securing funding.

3. Be Innovative and Creative

Fundraisers and grantmakers receive a large number of proposals on a regular basis, which can make it difficult for your proposal to stand out. By being innovative and creative in your approach to grant writing, you can increase your chances of success and differentiate yourself from the competition.

This may involve incorporating visual elements, such as infographics or videos, into your proposal, or using storytelling techniques to engage and inspire your audience.

4. Emphasize Sustainability

Funders are often interested in supporting projects that are sustainable and can have a lasting impact over time. When developing your grant proposal, it's important to emphasize the sustainability of your project, and to outline the steps that will be taken to ensure its long-term success.

This may involve developing a detailed sustainability plan, identifying sources of ongoing funding or support, or outlining the steps that will be taken to ensure the continued engagement of community members or stakeholders.

By following these tips and strategies, and by developing a clear and compelling proposal that aligns with the funder's priorities and values, you can increase your chances of success in securing funding for your organization or project.

5. Research Funding Opportunities

Before submitting a grant proposal, it's important to thoroughly research potential funding opportunities to ensure that your project aligns with the funder's priorities and goals. This may involve reviewing the funder's mission statement, program guidelines, and previously funded projects to get a better sense of their priorities and values.

By conducting thorough research, you can ensure that your grant proposal is a good fit for the funder, and increase your chances of success in securing funding.

6. Develop a Detailed Budget

A well-developed budget is a critical component of any grant proposal. When developing your budget, it's important to be realistic and to ensure that all costs are accounted for, including both direct and indirect expenses.

This may involve developing a detailed line-item budget, outlining the specific expenses that will be covered by the grant funding, and identifying other sources of revenue or in-kind support that will be used to supplement the grant.

By developing a clear and detailed budget, you can demonstrate your organization's financial responsibility and increase your chances of success in securing funding.

7. Review and Revise Your Proposal

Before submitting your grant proposal, it's important to review and revise it carefully to ensure that it is clear, compelling, and free from errors or inconsistencies.

This may involve seeking feedback from colleagues or other professionals in the field, as well as conducting a thorough review of the proposal to ensure that it meets all of the funder's requirements and addresses their priorities and values.

By taking the time to review and revise your proposal carefully, you can increase your chances of success in securing funding and ensure that your project has the greatest possible impact.

8. Follow Up with Funders

After submitting your grant proposal, it's important to follow up with the funder to ensure that they have received your proposal and to inquire about the status of your application.

This may involve sending a brief email or making a phone call to the funder, or attending networking events or other professional gatherings to connect with funders and other professionals in the field.

By following up with funders, you can demonstrate your commitment to your project and your willingness to engage with funders and other stakeholders to ensure its success.

9. Implement and Evaluate Your Project

If your grant proposal is successful, it's important to implement your project effectively and to evaluate its success to ensure that you are meeting your goals and objectives.

This may involve developing a detailed project plan and timeline, engaging with stakeholders and partners to ensure buy-in and support, and monitoring and evaluating your project's progress throughout its implementation.

By effectively implementing and evaluating your project, you can demonstrate your organization's capacity to manage and deliver impactful projects, and increase your chances of securing funding in the future.

10. Build and Maintain Relationships with Funders and Other Stakeholders

Finally, it's important to build and maintain strong relationships with funders and other stakeholders throughout the grant writing process and beyond. This may involve attending networking events, participating in professional associations or online forums, and engaging in regular communication with funders and other partners.

By building and maintaining strong relationships, you can increase your organization's visibility and reputation, demonstrate your commitment to your project and the wider community, and increase your chances of success in securing funding in the future.

Researching Grant Opportunities

Researching grant opportunities is an essential first step in the grant writing process.

It involves identifying potential funders, understanding their priorities and requirements, and assessing whether your organization and project align with their mission and goals.

Here are some key steps to follow when researching grant opportunities:

1. Identify Potential Funders

The first step in researching grant opportunities is to identify potential funders that may be a good fit for your organization and project.

This may involve searching online databases, such as the Foundation Center or Grants.gov, or exploring the websites of individual funders to learn more about their funding priorities and application requirements.

It's important to keep in mind that not all funders will be a good fit for your organization or project, so it's essential to carefully assess whether a potential funder's priorities and requirements align with your goals and objectives.

2. Read and Understand the Funder's Guidelines

Once you have identified potential funders, it's important to carefully read and understand their guidelines and application requirements. This may involve reviewing detailed instructions on how to apply, as well as information on the funder's priorities, funding levels, and eligibility requirements.

Pay close attention to the funder's guidelines, as failing to follow their instructions and requirements can result in your application being rejected.

3. Assess Your Organization's Eligibility

Before applying for a grant, it's important to assess your organization's eligibility to receive funding from the funder in question.

This may involve reviewing the funder's eligibility requirements, which may include factors such as the size and scope of your organization, your geographic location, and the types of programs or services you offer.

Ensure that your organization has the capacity to effectively manage and implement a grant-funded project, as funders will be looking for evidence of your organization's track record of success.

4. Identify Your Project's Alignment with the Funder's Priorities

When researching grant opportunities, it's essential to assess how your project aligns with the funder's priorities and mission. This may involve reviewing the funder's funding priorities and strategic objectives, and identifying areas where your project can make a meaningful impact.

Clearly articulate how your project aligns with the funder's priorities and objectives, and to provide evidence of the potential impact and outcomes of your proposed project.

5. Develop a Relationship with the Funder

Develop a relationship with the funder, particularly if you are seeking large or ongoing funding. This may involve reaching out to program officers or other representatives of the funder, attending informational sessions or webinars, and participating in professional associations or online forums.

By developing a relationship with the funder, you can increase your organization's visibility and reputation, demonstrate your commitment to your project and the wider community, and increase your chances of success in securing funding in the future.

What are the databases for grant research?

When researching grant opportunities, one of the best ways to identify potential funders is to use grant databases.

These are online resources that allow you to search for funding opportunities by category, location, funding amount, and other criteria.

Some of the most popular grant databases include:

1. Foundation Directory Online (FDO)

FDO is a comprehensive database of more than 140,000 grantmakers, which includes private foundations, community foundations, and corporate giving programs. It also includes detailed information on more than 11 million grants awarded by these funders, making it an excellent resource for researching grant opportunities and learning more about a funder's priorities and history.

FDO offers several subscription options, ranging from basic access to the database to more advanced features such as personalized recommendations and custom reports.

2. Grants.gov

Grants.gov is a database of federal funding opportunities, which includes more than 1,000 grant programs across 26 federal agencies. It allows users to search for grant opportunities by agency, category, funding type, and eligibility criteria.

Grants.gov also offers a range of tools and resources to help applicants navigate the federal grant application process, including a step-by-step guide to submitting an application and a list of frequently asked questions.

3. The Catalog of Federal Domestic Assistance (CFDA)

The CFDA is a comprehensive database of all federal programs that provide financial or non-financial assistance to individuals, organizations, and state and local governments. It includes more than 2,000 programs from over 200 federal agencies, and provides detailed information on eligibility criteria, funding amounts, and application requirements.

The CFDA is a valuable resource for those looking for federal grant opportunities, as well as those looking for other forms of government assistance such as loans and technical assistance.

4. The Foundation Center

The Foundation Center is a nonprofit organization that provides a range of resources and services to support the work of nonprofit organizations, including a comprehensive database of more than 100,000 grantmakers. It also offers a range of other resources, including webinars, workshops, and consulting services.

The Foundation Center's database is available through a subscription, and includes detailed information on grantmakers' funding priorities, giving history, and application requirements.

5. GuideStar

GuideStar is a database of more than 2.7 million nonprofit organizations, which includes detailed information on each organization's finances, governance, and mission. It is an excellent resource for researching potential partners or collaborators, as well as for learning more about potential funders.

GuideStar's basic search function is free, but more advanced features, such as access to financial information,

require a subscription.

6. Grant Station

Grant Station is a comprehensive database of private grantmakers and provides grantseekers with access to over 5,000 current funding opportunities.

In addition, Grant Station provides training, tools, and support to help grantseekers become successful fundraisers.

Grant Station offers multiple subscription options and is an excellent resource for small and mid-sized nonprofit organizations, as well as individual grantseekers.

7. Corporate Giving Network

The Corporate Giving Network is a database of corporate giving programs, which includes information on more than 5,000 companies and their giving programs. This database provides detailed information on each company's giving priorities and funding amounts, making it an excellent resource for nonprofit organizations seeking funding from the corporate sector.

The Corporate Giving Network offers a subscription corporate giving program.

8. State and Regional Grant Databases

In addition to national grant databases, many states and regions have their own grant databases that provide information on funding opportunities specific to that area. These databases may be managed by state agencies, nonprofit organizations, or other entities.

For example, the Arizona Community Foundation manages a grant database that provides information on funding opportunities available in Arizona. The Minnesota Council of Nonprofits manages a similar database that provides information on funding opportunities in Minnesota.

To find state and regional grant databases, search online for the name of your state or region and "grant database."

9. Pivot

Pivot is a comprehensive database of funding opportunities that includes grants, fellowships, awards, and other funding sources from around the world. It allows users to search for funding opportunities based on their research interests, career level, and other criteria.

Pivot is available through a subscription service, and provides a range of additional resources to support the grantseeking process.

Developing Strong Grant Proposals

Crafting a strong grant proposal is a critical step in securing funding for your organization's projects and programs. A well-written proposal can help you stand out among a crowded field of applicants and demonstrate your organization's ability to effectively carry out your proposed project.

Here are some key strategies for developing a strong grant proposal:

1. **Start with a Clear and Compelling Project Description**

   The project description is the heart of your grant proposal, and it should be both clear and compelling. Start by clearly outlining the need or problem that your project aims to address, and provide evidence to support your claims.

   Next, describe the specific activities and outcomes of your proposed project, as well as how you plan to measure and evaluate its success. Be sure to make a strong case for why your organization is uniquely qualified to carry out this project.

2. **Align Your Proposal with the Funder's Priorities**

   One of the most important aspects of developing a strong grant proposal is ensuring that it aligns with the priorities of the funder you are applying to.

   This means doing your research to understand the funder's mission, goals, and specific areas of interest. Use this information to tailor your proposal to their specific priorities and goals, highlighting how your proposed project aligns with their mission.

3. Develop a Realistic Budget

A strong grant proposal should include a detailed and realistic budget that clearly outlines the costs associated with your proposed project. Make sure your budget aligns with your proposed activities and is consistent with the funder's requirements. Include all relevant costs, including staff time, materials, and other expenses.

4. Provide Evidence of Your Organization's Capacity

In addition to outlining your proposed project, your grant proposal should also provide evidence of your organization's capacity to effectively carry out the project.

This includes information on your organization's past experience with similar projects, as well as any relevant partnerships, staff expertise, and other resources. Make sure to highlight your organization's strengths and expertise, and provide evidence to back up your claims.

5. Write a Clear and Compelling Narrative

Write a clear and compelling narrative that tells the story of your proposed project and makes a compelling case for why your organization is the best fit for this funding opportunity. This means using clear, concise language and avoiding jargon or technical terms that may be unfamiliar to the funder. Use concrete examples and stories to illustrate the impact of your proposed project, and make sure to answer any questions or concerns that the funder may have.

:

Once you have identified a funding opportunity that fits your organization's mission and goals, it's time to start developing your grant proposal. A well-crafted proposal can make the difference between receiving funding and being rejected, so it's important to invest time and effort into this step.

Here are some key steps to follow when developing a strong grant proposal:

1. **Review the grant guidelines:** Before you start writing, it's essential to carefully review the grant guidelines provided by the funding organization. This will ensure that you are addressing all of the requirements and expectations for the grant proposal. Make note of any page limits, formatting guidelines, or other specific instructions that must be followed.
2. **Develop a clear and compelling narrative**: The narrative section of your grant proposal is where you make your case for why your organization deserves funding. This section should clearly articulate your organization's mission and goals, and explain how the proposed project will help advance those objectives. Use strong, descriptive language and storytelling techniques to engage the reader and create a sense of urgency around the issue you are addressing.
3. **Provide data and evidence**: In addition to a compelling narrative, it's important to back up your claims with data and evidence. This might include statistics, research studies, or other relevant information that demonstrates the need for the proposed project and the potential impact it could have. Be sure to cite your sources and provide clear explanations of how the data supports your proposal.

4. **Clearly outline your project plan**: The grant proposal should clearly outline the steps you will take to implement the project, including timelines, budgets, and staffing plans. It's important to be specific and detailed, so that the funder can understand exactly how the project will be carried out. Be sure to include any potential challenges or roadblocks, and explain how you will address them.
5. **Include a sustainability plan**: Many grant funders are interested in ensuring that the projects they fund will have a lasting impact beyond the grant period. To address this, it's important to include a sustainability plan that outlines how the project will be continued or maintained after the grant funding ends. This might include plans for ongoing fundraising, partnerships with other organizations, or strategies for engaging community stakeholders.
6. **Proofread and edit:** Finally, it's essential to carefully proofread and edit your grant proposal before submitting it. Typos, grammatical errors, or formatting issues can detract from the strength of your proposal, so take the time to carefully review and revise your work. Consider having a colleague or professional editor review your proposal as well, to provide an additional perspective and catch any errors you may have missed.

Building Relationships with Funders

As a grant writer, building strong relationships with funders is an essential part of your job. The more connections and relationships you have, the more likely you are to secure funding for your organization.

In this section, we'll discuss the importance of building relationships with funders and provide some tips on how to do so effectively.

Why Building Relationships with Funders Matters

Building relationships with funders is crucial for several reasons. First, it allows you to better understand the goals and priorities of the funder, which can help you tailor your grant proposal to their needs.

By taking the time to get to know the funder, you can make sure that your proposal aligns with their mission and funding priorities, increasing your chances of receiving funding.

Second, building relationships with funders can help you stay top-of-mind when it comes to funding opportunities. When you have an established relationship with a funder, they are more likely to reach out to you when new funding opportunities arise or when they have additional funds to distribute.

Finally, building relationships with funders can help you establish a long-term partnership that goes beyond the grant award. By maintaining contact with the funder throughout the grant period, you can update them on the progress of your project and build a stronger relationship that could lead to future funding opportunities.

Tips for Building Relationships with Funders

Now that we've discussed the importance of building relationships with funders, let's dive into some tips for doing so effectively.

1. **Research the funder**. Before you reach out to a funder, take the time to research their mission, funding priorities, and past grant awards. This information can help you tailor your proposal to their needs and demonstrate your knowledge of their organization.

2. **Attend events and meetings**. Whenever possible, attend events and meetings where funders will be present. This could include conferences, seminars, or networking events. These events provide an opportunity to meet funders in person and establish a personal connection.
3. **Communicate regularly**. Once you have established a relationship with a funder, make sure to communicate with them regularly. This could include sending them updates on your project, inviting them to events or activities, or simply reaching out to check in.
4. **Follow up after receiving funding**. After receiving funding, make sure to follow up with the funder to express your gratitude and update them on the progress of your project. This can help solidify your relationship and position you for future funding opportunities.
5. **Be transparent and honest**. Building a strong relationship with a funder requires transparency and honesty. Be clear about your project goals, challenges, and progress, and don't be afraid to ask for feedback or advice.
6. **Be respectful of the funder's time**. While it's important to communicate regularly with funders, it's also important to be respectful of their time. Make sure your communications are concise and to the point, and avoid bombarding them with unnecessary updates or requests.

Budgeting for Grant Proposals: Best Practices and Strategies

Budgeting is an essential component of the grant proposal process. It shows funders that you have a clear understanding of the project's financial needs and that you have developed a plan for effectively using their resources.

When applying for a grant, one of the most crucial components of your proposal is the budget. Funders want to see a well-planned and well-thought-out budget that demonstrates how their funds will be used effectively and efficiently. A budget is not only a financial plan for your project, but also a tool to help you identify and manage the resources you will need to carry out your project.

Developing a budget for a grant proposal can be intimidating, but it doesn't have to be. By following some best practices and strategies, you can create a budget that will impress funders and improve your chances of receiving the grant.

In this section, we will explore some of the best practices and strategies for developing a budget that will strengthen your grant proposal.

1. Read the guidelines carefully

Before you start working on your budget, read the grant guidelines carefully. Make sure you understand the funding priorities and restrictions, and any budget-related requirements, such as matching funds or cost-sharing. These guidelines will provide you with the framework for creating a budget that aligns with the funder's goals.

2. Include all relevant costs

Your budget should include all costs associated with your project. This includes direct costs, such as salaries, equipment, supplies, and travel, as well as indirect costs, such as overhead and administrative expenses. Be sure to include both one-time and ongoing costs. If you are unsure about any costs, reach out to the funder for clarification.

3. Be realistic

It's important to be realistic when developing your budget. Avoid overestimating or underestimating costs, as this can make your proposal seem unprofessional or ill-prepared. Research the costs of the items and services you need, and use quotes or estimates from vendors and suppliers to support your budget figures.

4. Justify your expenses

When presenting your budget, make sure to provide a clear and detailed explanation of each expense. This will help the funder understand why the expense is necessary and how it will support your project's goals.

You should also indicate which expenses are essential to the project's success and which could be scaled back if necessary.

5. Show how the grant will be used

Your budget should clearly demonstrate how the grant funds will be used to support the project. This can be accomplished through a line-item budget or a narrative budget that explains how the grant will be used to cover specific expenses. Either way, the budget should be directly tied to the project goals and should show how the grant will be used to achieve those goals.

6. Get feedback

Once you have created a draft of your budget, share it with colleagues or advisors who can provide feedback. They may be able to identify areas where you could reduce costs or where you need to add more detail. You should also review the budget carefully yourself, checking for errors or inconsistencies.

7. **Review and revise**

Before submitting your proposal, make sure to review your budget and make any necessary revisions. You want to ensure that your budget is accurate, clear, and aligned with the funder's guidelines and priorities. Once you submit your proposal, you may not have the opportunity to revise your budget, so it's important to get it right the first time.

Creating Impactful Data and Evaluation Plans

As a grant writer, it is important to understand the significance of data and evaluation in the grant proposal process. Funders are always interested in the impact of the projects they fund and how the funds are being utilized.

Developing an effective data and evaluation plan can make the difference in the success of a grant proposal.

In this section, we will explore the best practices and strategies for creating impactful data and evaluation plans.

1. **Understand the funder's expectations**: Before you begin developing a data and evaluation plan, it is important to understand the funder's expectations. Read the grant guidelines carefully and identify what data the funder requires to demonstrate the impact of your project. The funder may ask for specific data points or may require you to measure certain outcomes.
2. **Develop SMART objectives**: The first step in developing a data and evaluation plan is to identify the objectives of your

project. It is important to develop SMART (Specific, Measurable, Achievable, Relevant, and Time-bound) objectives that can be measured effectively. SMART objectives help to ensure that your project goals are clear and that you can demonstrate the impact of your project.

3. **Identify data sources**: Once you have identified the objectives of your project, the next step is to identify the data sources that will help you measure the impact of your project. These data sources can include surveys, interviews, focus groups, and other methods. It is important to choose data sources that are appropriate for the project and can provide the necessary information.

4. **Develop data collection methods**: After identifying data sources, it is important to develop data collection methods that are effective and efficient. The data collection methods should align with the data sources identified and be designed to gather the necessary data. It is also important to ensure that the data collection methods are feasible and cost-effective.

5. **Use qualitative and quantitative data**: Both qualitative and quantitative data are important in demonstrating the impact of your project. Qualitative data includes narratives, stories, and case studies, while quantitative data includes statistics, numbers, and measurable data. Using a combination of qualitative and quantitative data helps to provide a comprehensive view of the impact of your project.

6. **Develop an evaluation plan**: The evaluation plan should outline how the data will be collected, analyzed, and reported. The plan should include a timeline for data collection, a description of the data analysis methods, and a summary of how the data will be reported to the funder. It is important to ensure that the evaluation plan aligns with the grant guidelines and the funder's expectations.

7. **Include feedback mechanisms**: Feedback mechanisms are important for gathering information about the impact of

your project and improving the project over time. The feedback mechanisms can include surveys, interviews, focus groups, and other methods. It is important to include feedback mechanisms in the evaluation plan and to ensure that the feedback is used to improve the project.

8. **Ensure the data is accurate and reliable**: This can be achieved by using standardized data collection methods, ensuring that the data is entered accurately, and verifying the data before it is analyzed. It is also important to ensure that the data is stored securely and that any personal information is protected.

Collaborating With Partners: Strategies For Successful Collaborative

Grant proposals often require collaboration among multiple partners to achieve common goals. Collaborative proposals can be an effective way to leverage the strengths and resources of different organizations, increase the impact of the project, and satisfy the funding agency's requirements for community engagement and collaboration.

However, collaboration also brings its own set of challenges and requires careful planning and execution to ensure success.

In this section, we will explore the strategies and best practices for creating successful collaborative grant proposals.

- **Identify the Right Partners:** The first step in successful collaboration is to identify the right partners for your project. Consider partners who bring complementary strengths, resources, and perspectives to the project. Identify partners who share your goals and values and who have a track record of successful collaboration. Look for partners who can contribute to the project in meaningful ways, such as providing expertise, access to populations, or funding.

- **Define Roles and Responsibilities:** Clear communication and well-defined roles and responsibilities are critical to successful collaboration. Each partner should have a clearly defined role in the project, and expectations for each partner's contributions should be spelled out in advance. The lead organization should take responsibility for coordinating the collaboration and ensuring that each partner is aware of their role and responsibilities.

- **Establish Trust and Communication:** Collaboration requires trust and open communication among partners. Take the time to build relationships and establish trust among partners before beginning the project. Regular communication among partners is critical to ensuring that everyone stays on the same page and can address any issues that arise in a timely manner.

- **Create a Shared Vision and Strategy**: Create a shared vision and strategy for the project that is agreed upon by all partners. The vision should be clear and compelling, and the strategy should outline the steps that each partner will take to achieve the project's goals. It is also important to establish a timeline for the project and to identify any potential roadblocks that may arise.

- Develop a Budget and Fundraising Strategy; Develop a budget and fundraising strategy that takes into account the resources and strengths of each partner. Each partner should be responsible for contributing to the project in a meaningful way, whether it is through funding, in-kind contributions, or other resources. It is important to establish a clear understanding of each partner's financial commitment to the project and to ensure that the budget is realistic and feasible.

- **Build in Evaluation and Feedback Mechanisms**: Evaluation and feedback mechanisms are critical to successful collaboration. Each partner should be responsible for providing regular updates on their progress and for sharing any challenges or issues that arise. Establish regular check-ins among partners and build in evaluation and feedback mechanisms to ensure that the project stays on track and that partners can learn from one another.

Part 4

Mastering Grant writing skills

Congratulations! You've made it to Part 4 of the book, which is all about mastering grant writing skills.

This section of the book is designed to help you take your grant writing to the next level, whether you're a beginner or an experienced grant writer.

In this section, we'll explore some advanced topics and strategies that will help you improve your grant writing skills, stay up-to-date with the latest trends and best practices, and increase your chances of success.

1. **Writing Winning Proposals**

   One of the most critical skills to master in grant writing is the ability to write winning proposals. A winning proposal is one that is clear, concise, and compelling. It should make a strong case for your project or program and demonstrate its potential to make a meaningful impact. A winning proposal should also be well-organized, easy to read, and free of errors.

   To write a winning proposal, you should start by carefully reading the funder's guidelines and requirements. Make sure you understand what the funder is looking for and what they expect to see in a proposal. Then, craft a strong introduction that clearly and concisely outlines your project's purpose and its potential impact.

   Use evidence and data to support your claims and make a compelling case for your project. Be sure to include a well-thought-out budget that accurately reflects the costs of your project.

2. **Using Storytelling in Grant Writing**

Storytelling is an essential tool in grant writing. Telling a compelling story can help you engage the reader, make an emotional connection, and illustrate the impact of your project. Use anecdotes, case studies, and personal stories to bring your project to life and help the funder see the value of your work. Use vivid language and sensory details to paint a picture of your project and its potential impact. Don't be afraid to be creative and use storytelling to your advantage.

3. **Professional Development for Grant Writers**

Staying up-to-date with the latest trends and best practices in grant writing is critical to your success. Professional development opportunities, such as conferences, workshops, and webinars, can help you stay current and improve your skills. They can also help you build a network of peers and connect with funders, which can be invaluable in your grant writing career. Take advantage of these opportunities to stay ahead of the curve and increase your chances of success.

4. **Peer Review and Editing**

Getting feedback on your grant proposals is essential. Peer review and editing can help you identify areas for improvement, catch errors and inconsistencies, and ensure that your proposal is clear and concise. Find a trusted colleague, mentor, or writing group to review your proposal and provide feedback. Be open to their suggestions and use their feedback to improve your proposal.

5. **Tracking and Measuring Your Success**

Once you've submitted your proposal, it's essential to track and measure your success. Track your progress and use data to demonstrate the impact of your project. Use this information to make improvements and refine your approach. Be sure to communicate your success to your funders and stakeholders, and use it to build momentum for your next project.

Overcoming Writer's Block and other Writing Challenges

Grant writing can be a challenging process, especially when you hit a wall with writer's block. However, it is essential to learn how to overcome these challenges and keep the momentum going in your writing.

In this section, we will discuss some common writing challenges that grant writers face and strategies for overcoming them.

1. **Writer's block**: Writer's block is a common challenge that can happen to any writer, whether experienced or new. Writer's block occurs when a writer is unable to come up with new ideas or put words down on paper. This can be frustrating, especially when deadlines are approaching. There are several strategies that grant writers can use to overcome writer's block.

   One of the most effective ways to overcome writer's block is to take a break. Taking a break allows you to clear your mind and come back with a fresh perspective. Take a walk, listen to music, read a book, or do anything that helps you relax and get your mind off of writing.

Additionally, you can try brainstorming to generate new ideas, or change your writing environment to something new and exciting.

2. **Procrastination**: Procrastination is another challenge that grant writers may face. Procrastination happens when you delay starting a writing project or delay completing it, despite having the time to do so. Procrastination can lead to missed deadlines and a lower quality of work.

   To overcome procrastination, set realistic deadlines for yourself and make a plan to stick to them. Break the writing project into small, manageable tasks and set goals for completing them. More so, eliminate any distractions that may be taking up your time, and create a dedicated workspace for writing.

3. **Fear of rejection**: Another challenge that grant writers may face is a fear of rejection. Writing a grant proposal is a long and challenging process, and the fear of rejection can be daunting. However, it is essential to remember that rejection is a part of the process.

   To overcome the fear of rejection, it is crucial to have a growth mindset. View the process of grant writing as an opportunity to learn and improve your writing skills. Additionally, seek feedback from peers or colleagues to help you improve your writing.

4. **Writing style**: Grant writers must write in a way that is both informative and persuasive. Writing style can be a challenge for some writers, especially those who are new to grant writing.

To improve your writing style, it is essential to understand the audience that you are writing for. Tailor your writing to fit the needs of the funder, and use language that is clear, concise, and easy to understand. Additionally, use active voice and avoid jargon or overly technical terms.

5. **Time management**: Time management can be a significant challenge for grant writers, especially when juggling multiple writing projects. Time management is critical in ensuring that deadlines are met and that the quality of the work is not compromised.

   To manage your time effectively, create a schedule that prioritizes the most critical tasks. Set realistic deadlines for yourself, and make sure to give yourself enough time to complete each task. Additionally, use a timer to keep track of your progress and eliminate any distractions that may be taking up your time.

Developing Effective Cover Letters and Executive Summaries

Developing effective cover letters and executive summaries is crucial to the success of any grant proposal. These sections serve as the first impression of your proposal and should be carefully crafted to engage the reader and convey the essence of your project.

In this section, we will discuss best practices and strategies for creating compelling cover letters and executive summaries that effectively communicate the value of your proposal.

1. **Understanding the Purpose of Cover Letters and Executive Summaries**

   Cover letters and executive summaries serve different purposes but are equally important in any grant proposal. The cover letter is the first communication between the grant writer and the funder, providing an opportunity to introduce the proposal and create a favorable impression. It should be written in a clear and concise manner, highlighting the essential aspects of your proposal, including its purpose, objectives, and expected outcomes.

   The executive summary, on the other hand, provides a brief overview of the entire proposal, highlighting the key points and the expected impact of the project. It should be written in a way that captures the attention of the reader and motivates them to read the full proposal. An effective executive summary should convey the significance of the project, its potential impact, and the qualifications of the team.

2. **Crafting a Compelling Cover Letter**

   The cover letter should be concise, but it should also capture the essence of your proposal. Here are some tips to help you craft an effective cover letter:

- Address the funder directly and introduce yourself and your organization briefly.
- Explain the purpose of the grant and how it aligns with the mission and goals of the funder.
- Provide a brief summary of the project, including its objectives and expected outcomes.
- Highlight the qualifications and expertise of your team in implementing the proposed project.

- Express your gratitude for the opportunity to apply for the grant and your willingness to provide additional information if needed.
- Close the letter by inviting the funder to contact you if they have any questions or require more information.
3. Creating an Impactful Executive Summary

The executive summary is your chance to make a strong case for your proposal.

Here are some tips to help you craft an effective executive summary:

- Start with a clear and concise statement of the problem your project aims to address.
- Highlight the significance of the project and its potential impact on the target population.
- Provide a brief overview of the project, including the methods you will use to achieve the objectives and the expected outcomes.
- Clearly outline the qualifications and expertise of the team members involved in the project.
- State the amount of funding requested and provide a brief budget overview.
- Close the executive summary by expressing your gratitude for the opportunity to apply for the grant and your willingness to provide additional information if needed.
4. Editing and Proofreading

Once you have written your cover letter and executive summary, it is essential to edit and proofread carefully to ensure that your writing is clear, concise, and free from errors. Here are some tips to help you:

- Take a break before editing to clear your mind and help you approach the writing with a fresh perspective.
- Read your writing aloud to catch any awkward phrasing or grammatical errors.
- Use spell-check and grammar-check software to identify and correct errors.
- Have a colleague or mentor review your writing to provide feedback and help you identify areas that need improvement.

Practical example of a cover letter for a grant proposal:

[Your Name]
[Your Organization]
[Your Address]
[City, State ZIP Code]
[Email Address]
[Phone Number]
[Date]

[Grant Officer Name]
[Grant Officer Title]
[Grant-Making Organization Name]
[Grant-Making Organization Address]
[City, State ZIP Code]

Dear [Grant Officer Name],

I am writing to express my enthusiasm and interest in the [Grant Program Name] grant opportunity offered by [Grant-Making Organization Name]. Our organization, [Your Organization Name], is a nonprofit that has been dedicated to [your organization's mission] for over [number of years] years.

We believe that the goals and objectives of the [Grant Program Name] align well with our mission and strategic vision. The grant funds would allow us to expand our reach and impact, and to better serve the community we work with.

We plan to use the grant funds to [briefly describe your proposed project or program, highlighting how it will align with the grant program's goals and objectives]. We have a highly experienced team with a track record of success, and we are confident that our proposed project will make a significant positive impact in our community.

Thank you for considering our application. We look forward to hearing from you.

Sincerely,

[Your Name]

Example of an Executive Summary:

Executive Summary

Project Title: Increasing Access to Healthy Foods in Underserved Communities

Project Overview:

Our organization, Healthy Community Solutions, is proposing a project that aims to increase access to healthy foods in underserved communities. Our target communities have limited access to fresh fruits and vegetables, which contributes to high rates of obesity and diet-related chronic diseases.

Many low-income communities in our region lack access to healthy foods, contributing to high rates of obesity and diet-related chronic diseases. This problem is exacerbated by the limited availability of grocery stores and fresh produce in these communities. As a result, residents rely heavily on unhealthy processed foods and sugary drinks, which leads to negative health outcomes and reduced quality of life.

Healthy Community Solutions is excited to propose this project and make a positive impact on the health and well-being of underserved communities in our region. We believe that our approach, which includes building partnerships, engaging community members, and providing nutrition education, will lead to sustainable improvements

in community health outcomes.

Project Goals:

1. *Increase access to fresh, healthy foods in underserved communities.*
2. *Improve community health outcomes by reducing rates of obesity and diet-related chronic diseases.*
3. *Provide nutrition education and cooking classes to encourage healthy eating habits.*

The project will consist of the following activities:

1. *Establishing partnerships with local farmers to provide fresh produce to underserved communities at affordable prices.*

2. *Building community gardens in underserved neighborhoods to increase access to fresh produce.*
3. *Providing nutrition education and cooking classes to community members to encourage healthy eating habits.*
4. *Establishing a mobile market to bring fresh produce to communities with limited access to grocery stores.*

The project will be implemented over a period of two years and will benefit approximately 5,000 individuals in underserved communities.

The proposed project will have a significant impact on the health and well-being of underserved communities in our region. By increasing access to fresh produce and providing nutrition education, we expect to see improvements in community health outcomes, including reduced rates of obesity and diet-related chronic diseases. Additionally, the project will support local farmers and build stronger community connections through partnerships and community engagement.

The total budget for this project is $500,000 over two years. Funding will be used to cover the cost of building community gardens, establishing partnerships with local farmers, providing nutrition education and cooking classes, and purchasing a mobile market.

Writing Winning Letters of Inquiry: Strategies for Effective Pre Proposal communication

Writing a strong letter of inquiry is an essential part of grant writing, as it provides a brief overview of your project to the potential funder before submitting a full proposal. It serves as an initial point of contact, and can often be the key to securing a grant. While there is no one-size-fits-all approach to writing a successful letter of inquiry, there are some strategies that can help you make the most of this important communication tool.

1. **Do your research**: Before writing your letter of inquiry, take the time to research the potential funder and their funding priorities. This will help you determine whether your project is a good fit for their organization, and can help you tailor your letter accordingly. Look for any guidelines or requirements for submitting letters of inquiry, and make sure to follow them closely.

2. **Keep it concise**: Your letter of inquiry should be brief, typically no more than two pages. It should provide a clear and concise overview of your project, highlighting its key components and potential impact. Avoid getting bogged down in details or technical jargon, and focus on making a strong case for why your project is worthy of funding.

3. **Use a compelling opening**: The opening of your letter of inquiry should grab the reader's attention and clearly articulate the purpose of your project. This could be a personal anecdote, a surprising statistic, or a brief statement that highlights the problem your project aims to address. The goal is to engage the reader and make them want to learn more about your project.

4. **Demonstrate the need**: In order to secure funding, you need to convince the potential funder that your project is addressing a significant need. Use data, statistics, and other evidence to demonstrate the problem you are addressing, and explain why it is important. Make sure to connect the need to the potential impact of your project, and highlight the specific outcomes you hope to achieve.

5. **Focus on the solution**: Once you've demonstrated the need, it's time to focus on the solution. Explain how your project will address the need you've identified, and describe the specific activities or interventions you plan to undertake. Make sure to highlight any innovative or unique

aspects of your approach, and emphasize how it aligns with the potential funder's priorities.

6. **Provide a budget estimate**: While you don't need to provide a detailed budget in your letter of inquiry, it's important to provide a rough estimate of the total project cost. This will help the potential funder get a sense of the scale of your project, and can help them determine whether it fits within their funding priorities.

7. **Be clear about next steps**: Make sure to clearly articulate the next steps in the process. This could include submitting a full proposal, scheduling a follow-up call or meeting, or requesting additional information. Whatever the next steps are, be sure to express your enthusiasm for the potential partnership, and thank the funder for their time and consideration.

Practical example of letter of Inquiry

Dear [Funder's Name],

I hope this letter finds you well. I am writing to express my interest in the [Name of Grant Program] offered by [Funder's Name]. I have reviewed the guidelines and eligibility criteria, and I believe that our organization aligns well with the program's goals and objectives.

[Insert brief description of your organization and its mission.]

We are currently seeking funding to support a project that aims to [Insert brief project summary]. We have identified a clear need for this project in our community, and we believe it has the potential to make a significant impact.

[Include a brief explanation of how your project aligns with the goals of the funder and how it can contribute to achieving their objectives.]

We would greatly appreciate the opportunity to discuss our proposal in more detail with you. If you feel that our project would be a good fit for the [Name of Grant Program], we would be happy to provide additional information and answer any questions you may have.

Thank you for considering our letter of inquiry. We look forward to hearing from you soon.

Sincerely,

[Your Name]

[Your Title]

[Your Organization]

Part 5
Breaking into the Grant writing industry

Breaking into the grant writing industry can be challenging, but with the right mindset and strategies, it is possible to establish a career in this field.

Breaking into the grant writing industry takes time and effort, but with persistence and the right strategies, it is possible to establish a successful career in this field. Remember to keep learning and growing, and always look for opportunities to gain experience and build relationships with other professionals in the industry.

Here are some tips on how to break into the grant writing industry.

1. **Gain Experience**: To get started in grant writing, it is important to gain experience in the field. Look for volunteer opportunities at local non-profit organizations, schools or hospitals. These organizations often need grant writers to help them secure funding, and by volunteering, you can gain valuable experience.
2. **Attend Workshops and Conferences**: Attending workshops and conferences can be a great way to learn more about grant writing and network with other professionals in the field. Look for conferences and workshops in your area, or consider attending an online conference or webinar.
3. **Join Professional Organizations**: Joining a professional organization for grant writers can be a great way to connect with others in the field and stay up-to-date on the latest trends and best practices. Consider joining the Grant Professionals Association or the American Grant Writers' Association.

4. **Develop a Portfolio**: A portfolio of successful grant applications can help demonstrate your expertise and experience to potential employers. As you gain experience, be sure to keep a record of your successful applications, and ask permission to use them in your portfolio.
5. **Network with Peers**: Building relationships with other grant writers can help you learn about job opportunities and gain insights into the industry. Attend networking events, join online groups, and engage with others on social media platforms.
6. **Apply for Internships or Entry-Level Positions**: Applying for internships or entry-level positions at non-profit organizations, educational institutions or government agencies can be a great way to gain hands-on experience in the grant writing field.
7. **Leverage Transferable Skills**: If you have experience in a related field, such as marketing or communications, you may be able to leverage your transferable skills to break into grant writing. Highlighting these skills on your resume and cover letter can help demonstrate your potential value to potential employers.

Here are some additional topics and ideas that could be included in a discussion of "Breaking into the Grant Writing Industry":
1. **Networking strategies**: In order to succeed in the grant writing industry, it's important to build connections with other professionals in the field. This might involve attending industry conferences, joining professional organizations, or seeking out informational interviews with experienced grant writers.
2. **Developing a portfolio**: When applying for grant writing jobs, it's often helpful to have a portfolio of past work to share with potential employers. This could include writing samples, project proposals, and examples of successful grants that you have helped to secure.

3. **Freelancing vs. in-house positions:** There are many different types of grant writing positions, ranging from freelance or contract work to full-time, in-house positions. It's important to consider the pros and cons of each type of position when deciding where to focus your job search.

4. **Building your skills and expertise**: Even after you have landed your first grant writing job, it's important to continue developing your skills and building your expertise in the field. This might involve taking professional development courses, seeking out mentorship or coaching, or pursuing advanced degrees in a related field.

5. **Staying up-to-date with industry trends and best practices**: The grant writing industry is constantly evolving, so it's important to stay informed about the latest trends, best practices, and funding opportunities. This might involve following industry blogs, attending webinars or other professional development events, or subscribing to relevant publications or newsletters.

6. **Strategies for standing out in a competitive job market**: As with any industry, the grant writing field can be competitive, and it can be difficult to stand out among other qualified candidates. Some strategies for setting yourself apart might include developing a unique niche or area of expertise, building a strong online presence, or leveraging your personal or professional network.

7. **Finding mentorship and support:** Finally, it's important to remember that the grant writing industry can be challenging, and it's normal to face setbacks or obstacles along the way. Finding a mentor or support group of other grant writers can be a valuable way to stay motivated, gain new insights and perspectives, and navigate the ups and downs of the field.

Building a portfolio: Strategies for demonstrating your grant writing skills

Building a portfolio of successful grant proposals is an essential step for breaking into the grant writing industry. A strong portfolio can help demonstrate your skills as a grant writer and increase your chances of securing new opportunities.

Here are some strategies for building a portfolio that showcases your grant writing skills:

1. **Start by building a collection of proposals**: The first step to building a grant writing portfolio is to start accumulating a collection of successful proposals. You can use past proposals that you have written for organizations or create mock proposals that demonstrate your grant writing skills. Make sure to collect a range of proposals that showcase your ability to write for different types of grants and organizations.
2. **Highlight your successful proposals**: Once you have a collection of proposals, select the most successful ones to include in your portfolio. Choose proposals that have won grants, proposals that received high scores, or proposals that received positive feedback from reviewers. These proposals will help demonstrate your ability to write effective grant proposals and secure funding.
3. **Create a template for your portfolio**: To make your portfolio stand out, create a template that showcases your proposals in an organized and professional manner. Include a brief introduction that highlights your experience and qualifications as a grant writer, and then create sections for each of the proposals you will include. Make sure to include a brief summary of the proposal, the grant amount, and the funding organization.

4. **Tailor your portfolio to the job**: When applying for a grant writing position, it's essential to tailor your portfolio to the job you are applying for. Research the organization and the types of grants they typically fund, and select proposals from your collection that are similar in scope and focus. Make sure to highlight your experience writing proposals for similar organizations and demonstrate your understanding of the grant funding landscape.

5. **Include metrics and results**: In addition to showcasing your writing skills, make sure to include metrics and results in your portfolio. Include information on the success of the grants you have written, such as the number of people impacted by the funding or the specific goals that were achieved. Including metrics and results will help demonstrate your ability to not only write effective proposals but also achieve tangible results for the organizations you work with.

6. **Keep your portfolio up-to-date**: Make sure to keep your portfolio up-to-date with your most recent successful proposals. Continuously updating your portfolio will help demonstrate your ongoing success as a grant writer and increase your chances of securing new opportunities.

Practical examples of how to build a portfolio to demonstrate your grant writing skills:

1. **Create a mock grant proposal**: One way to demonstrate your grant writing skills is by creating a mock grant proposal. You can choose a topic that aligns with your interests and research funding opportunities for that topic. Once you have identified a suitable opportunity, you can develop a grant proposal that outlines the problem, proposed solution, budget, and evaluation plan. You can then use this proposal as a sample to demonstrate your writing skills.

2. **Volunteer as a grant writer**: Another way to build a portfolio is by volunteering as a grant writer. You can identify local nonprofit organizations or community groups that are in need of grant funding and offer your services as a volunteer grant writer. This will allow you to gain hands-on experience in grant writing, while also building a portfolio of successful grant applications.

3. **Create case studies**: You can also create case studies that highlight your grant writing skills. For example, if you have successfully secured funding for a nonprofit organization or community group, you can create a case study that outlines the problem, the grant application process, and the outcomes achieved as a result of the funding. This will allow potential clients or employers to see the impact of your grant writing skills.

4. **Develop a blog or writing samples**: You can create a blog or develop a collection of writing samples that showcase your grant writing skills. This can include articles, blog posts, or other written materials that demonstrate your ability to write persuasively and effectively. By sharing your writing online, you can also build a professional network and attract potential clients or employers.

Here's some more information on building a portfolio to demonstrate your grant writing skills:

When you're looking to break into the grant writing industry, having a strong portfolio can be an essential tool for demonstrating your skills and expertise to potential clients or employers. Your portfolio should showcase your best work and highlight your ability to craft compelling grant proposals that meet the needs of funders.

Here are some tips and examples to help you build an effective grant writing portfolio:

1. **Start with your best work:** Your portfolio should include only your strongest and most successful grant proposals. Be selective and choose projects that demonstrate your ability to write clear, concise, and compelling proposals that meet the needs of funders. Be sure to highlight any successful outcomes or achievements that resulted from your proposals.
2. **Include a variety of project types:** Your portfolio should showcase a range of different types of grant proposals. This can include proposals for different funding sources, such as government agencies, private foundations, or corporate philanthropy programs. You should also aim to include proposals for different project types, such as research studies, program development, or capacity building.
3. **Provide context**: Each proposal in your portfolio should include a brief summary that provides context for the project. This should include information on the funder, the purpose of the project, and any relevant background information or data. This will help potential clients or employers understand the scope and impact of your work.
4. **Highlight your unique skills and expertise:** If you have specialized skills or expertise in a particular area, such as program evaluation or community engagement, be sure to highlight this in your portfolio. You can include a brief bio or statement that highlights your experience and qualifications.
5. **Use visuals to enhance your portfolio**: Including visuals, such as charts, tables, or images, can help to break up the text and make your portfolio more engaging. Be sure to use visuals that are relevant to the project and help to illustrate the impact of your work.

Here are a few examples of successful grant writing portfolios:

1. **Portfolio Example 1**: This portfolio includes a variety of grant proposals for different types of projects, such as program development and research studies. Each proposal includes a brief summary that provides context for the project, as well as a section on outcomes and achievements. The portfolio also includes a section on the writer's qualifications and expertise in grant writing.
2. **Portfolio Example 2:** This portfolio includes a range of successful grant proposals for different types of funders, including government agencies and private foundations. Each proposal includes a section on the writer's role in the project, as well as a detailed description of the project's goals, methods, and outcomes. The portfolio also includes a section on the writer's experience and qualifications in grant writing.
3. **Portfolio Example 3**: This portfolio includes a variety of grant proposals for projects in different fields, such as education, health, and social services. Each proposal includes a section on the project's goals, methods, and outcomes, as well as a summary of the funder's requirements and priorities. The portfolio also includes a section on the writer's qualifications and experience in grant writing, as well as a list of relevant skills and expertise.

Fictional grant writer portfolio:

Name: Sarah Johnson

Contact Information:

- *Email: sarahj@email.com*
- *Phone: (555) 555-5555*
- *Website: sarahjgrantwriting.com*

Summary: Sarah Johnson is a skilled grant writer with over 10 years of experience in the nonprofit sector. She has a proven track record of securing funding for a range of organizations, from small local charities to large international NGOs. Her expertise includes grant research, proposal writing, and program evaluation. She is passionate about working with organizations that are making a positive impact in their communities.

Professional Experience:

Grant Writer, Community Foundation of Anytown, Anytown, USA

- *Conducted grant research and wrote proposals for a variety of local nonprofit organizations*
- *Maintained relationships with funders and community partners*
- *Worked closely with grantees to provide support and guidance on program evaluation*

Development Officer, International Relief Organization, Anytown, USA

- *Developed and implemented a comprehensive fundraising strategy*
- *Wrote successful grant proposals to secure funding from foundations and government agencies*
- *Coordinated events and donor cultivation efforts*

Grant Writer, Women's Shelter, Anytown, USA

- *Conducted grant research and wrote proposals for programs to support survivors of domestic violence*

- *Worked with program staff to develop and implement evaluation plans*
- *Assisted with other fundraising activities, including donor appeals and special events*

Education:

- *Bachelor of Arts in Sociology, Anytown University*
- *Certificate in Grant Writing, Anytown Nonprofit Training Center*

Skills:

- *Grant research*
- *Proposal writing*
- *Program evaluation*
- *Donor cultivation*
- *Event coordination*
- *Budgeting*

Samples:

- *Successful grant proposal for a local community health clinic*
- *Evaluation plan for a youth mentoring program*
- *Donor appeal letter for a women's shelter*

References: Available upon request.

Note: This is just a fictional example, and an actual grant writer portfolio may look different depending on the individual's experience, skills, and areas of focus.

Grant Writer Portfolio: John Smith

Contact Information: Email: johnsmith@email.com Phone: (555) 555-5555

Objective: To obtain a position as a grant writer for a nonprofit organization, utilizing my skills and experience in grant research, proposal writing, and project management.

Education: Master of Public Administration, University of California, Los Angeles (UCLA), 2015 Bachelor of Arts in Sociology, University of California, Berkeley, 2012

Professional Experience:

Grant Writer, Hope House (Los Angeles, CA), 2017-Present

- *Conducted grant research to identify potential funding opportunities for programs serving homeless individuals and families.*
- *Developed and submitted grant proposals to private foundations and government agencies, resulting in over $500,000 in awarded grants.*
- *Coordinated with program managers to develop program budgets and project plans for grant proposals.*
- *Managed a grant reporting process, including gathering and analyzing data, writing and submitting reports, and ensuring compliance with grant requirements.*

Development Coordinator, HealthFirst (San Francisco, CA), 2015-2017

- *Assisted in the planning and execution of fundraising events, resulting in a 20% increase in revenue from the previous year.*
- *Developed and implemented a donor recognition program, resulting in increased donor retention rates.*
- *Conducted research on prospective donors and assisted in the preparation of grant proposals for foundation and corporate giving programs.*

Volunteer Experience: Grant Writing Volunteer, Community Outreach Center (San Francisco, CA), 2014-2015

- *Conducted grant research and assisted in the preparation of grant proposals for programs serving low-income families and seniors.*

Skills:

- *Proficient in grant research and proposal writing, including familiarity with various grant databases and application systems.*
- *Experienced in project management, including budgeting, reporting, and compliance monitoring.*
- *Proficient in Microsoft Office suite, including Excel, Word, and PowerPoint.*
- *Excellent verbal and written communication skills, with experience in public speaking and donor communications.*

References: Available upon request.

Another fictional grant writer portfolio:

Name: Emily Johnson

Overview: Emily Johnson is an experienced grant writer with over 10 years of experience in securing funding for nonprofit organizations in the health and education sectors. Emily has a track record of success in securing grants from a variety of sources, including private foundations, government agencies, and corporations.

Professional Experience:

Grant Writer, XYZ Health Foundation, New York, NY (2016 – Present)

- *Research and identify grant opportunities for the organization*
- *Write grant proposals, letters of inquiry, and other fundraising materials*
- *Collaborate with program staff to gather data and information for proposals*
- *Manage grant reporting and compliance*

Grant Writer, ABC Education Nonprofit, San Francisco, CA (2011 – 2016)

- *Developed and implemented a comprehensive grant strategy for the organization*
- *Secured over $2 million in grant funding from foundations, corporations, and government agencies*
- *Conducted prospect research and cultivated relationships with potential funders*
- *Wrote and submitted grant proposals, reports, and other materials*

- *Coordinated with program staff to ensure programmatic alignment with grant-funded activities*

Freelance Grant Writer, Self-Employed (2008 – 2011)

- *Wrote and submitted grant proposals on behalf of various nonprofit organizations*
- *Conducted prospect research and provided guidance on grant strategy*
- *Helped organizations with grant reporting and compliance*

Key Skills:

- *Research and prospecting: Experienced in conducting research to identify grant opportunities and cultivate relationships with potential funders.*
- *Proposal development: Skilled in developing comprehensive and compelling grant proposals, letters of inquiry, and other fundraising materials.*
- *Collaboration: Proven ability to work collaboratively with program staff to gather data and information and ensure programmatic alignment with grant-funded activities.*
- *Project management: Strong project management skills, including the ability to manage multiple grants and reporting requirements.*
- *Communication: Excellent written and verbal communication skills, including the ability to present complex information in a clear and concise manner.*

Education:

- *Bachelor of Arts in English, University of California, Berkeley*
- *Certificate in Grant Writing, San Francisco State University*

Samples of Work:

- *XYZ Health Foundation Grant Proposal, submitted and awarded $500,000*
- *ABC Education Nonprofit Annual Report, including grant-funded activities*
- *Letter of Inquiry to the Bill and Melinda Gates Foundation, securing an invitation to submit a full proposal.*

Another fictional grant writer portfolio:

Name: Sarah Jackson

About me: I am a highly experienced grant writer with a passion for making a positive impact on the world through philanthropic initiatives. I have over 10 years of experience working in the non-profit sector and have successfully secured funding for a wide range of projects, from community development to environmental conservation.

Education and training:

- *Bachelor's degree in Nonprofit Management from the University of California, Los Angeles*
- *Certificate in Grant Writing from the Foundation Center*

Grant writing experience:

- *Secured a $500,000 grant from the National Science Foundation to support a research project on sustainable agriculture practices*

- *Successfully secured $250,000 in funding from the Environmental Protection Agency for a project on reducing greenhouse gas emissions in urban areas*
- *Worked with a team to secure $1 million in funding from the Bill and Melinda Gates Foundation for a project aimed at improving access to clean water in developing countries*
- *Developed a successful grant proposal for a local community center that secured $50,000 in funding from the United Way*

Skills:

- *Strong research and analysis skills, with the ability to identify potential grant opportunities and develop winning proposals*
- *Excellent writing and communication skills, with the ability to craft compelling narratives that effectively communicate the goals and objectives of a project*
- *Proven track record of building strong relationships with funders and community partners*
- *Ability to manage multiple projects and meet tight deadlines*

Portfolio:

- *Proposal for a community arts program, including detailed budget and evaluation plan*
- *Proposal for a research project on climate change, including data and analysis of potential impact*
- *Proposal for a youth mentorship program, including letters of support from community partners and program participants*
- *Cover letter and resume highlighting my experience and skills in grant writing*

References:

- *Jane Smith, Director of Development at ABC Nonprofit*
- *John Johnson, Program Officer at XYZ Foundation*
- *Sarah Brown, Executive Director at DEF Community Center*

Contact information: Email: sarahjackson@email.com Phone: (555) 555-5555 Website: www.sarahjacksongrantwriting.com

---

Another fictional grant writer portfolio:

Grant Writer Portfolio: John Smith

Introduction: I am a highly skilled and experienced grant writer with over 10 years of experience in securing funding for a variety of non-profit organizations. I have a proven track record of writing successful proposals for both government and private funding sources, and I am committed to making a positive impact in the communities I serve.

Writing Samples:

1. *Project Proposal for Youth Mentorship Program As a grant writer for the Youth Mentorship Program, I developed a proposal that secured $100,000 in funding from the Department of Health and Human Services. The proposal outlined a comprehensive mentorship program for at-risk youth in low-income communities, providing*

academic support, life skills training, and career guidance. The program served over 500 youth over three years and achieved a 95% success rate in high school graduation and college enrollment.

2. *Operating Budget Proposal for Local Food Bank As a grant writer for the Local Food Bank, I developed a proposal that secured $50,000 in funding from a private foundation. The proposal included an operating budget that ensured the food bank could continue to serve the needs of the community, including providing meals for low-income families, seniors, and individuals experiencing homelessness. The proposal highlighted the success of the food bank in distributing over 500,000 pounds of food annually, and emphasized the need for ongoing support to continue these efforts.*

3. *Proposal for Community Health Clinic Expansion As a grant writer for the Community Health Clinic, I developed a proposal that secured $250,000 in funding from the state government. The proposal outlined a plan for expanding the clinic's services, including hiring additional medical staff and purchasing new equipment. The expansion allowed the clinic to serve a larger population, including those without health insurance, and provided much-needed access to affordable healthcare in the community.*

Testimonials:

"John is an exceptional grant writer, with a keen ability to capture the essence of our organization and translate it into compelling proposals. He has been instrumental in securing funding for several of our most successful programs, and we look forward to working with him for years to come." - Maria Hernandez, Executive Director, Youth Mentorship Program

"John is a talented grant writer who always goes above and beyond to ensure our proposals are competitive and compelling. His attention to detail and knowledge of the grant writing process have been invaluable to our organization, and we are grateful for his contributions." - Michael Johnson, Executive Director, Local Food Bank

"John is an outstanding grant writer who is able to convey complex ideas and data in a way that is easy for funders to understand. His ability to develop successful proposals has been crucial to our organization's growth and success, and we are fortunate to have him on our team." - Sarah Lee, Executive Director, Community Health Clinic

Conclusion:

As a grant writer, I am committed to helping non-profit organizations secure the funding they need to make a positive impact in their communities. With a proven track record of successful grant writing, a deep understanding of the funding landscape, and a passion for creating change, I am confident that I can help your organization achieve its goals.

Another example of a grant writer portfolio:

Name: Emily Johnson

Experience:

- *3 years of experience in grant writing and development, with a focus on education and youth programs*

- *Successfully secured $500,000 in grant funding for a local non-profit organization*
- *Developed strong relationships with funders and community partners, resulting in increased funding and visibility for non-profit organizations*
- *Led grant writing training workshops for non-profit organizations and community groups*

Education:

- *Bachelor of Arts in English from the University of California, Los Angeles*
- *Master of Public Administration from the University of Southern California*

Skills:

- *Grant writing and proposal development*
- *Research and analysis*
- *Budgeting and financial management*
- *Relationship building and communication*
- *Data collection and analysis*
- *Project management*

Projects:

1. *Youth Empowerment Program Grant Proposal - Secured $250,000 in grant funding from the California Community Foundation for a local non-profit organization's youth empowerment program. Developed a comprehensive grant proposal outlining the program's goals, activities, and outcomes, and worked closely with the non-profit organization's leadership to ensure the proposal aligned with the organization's mission and vision.*

2. *School-Based Health Center Planning Grant Proposal -*
   Successfully secured $75,000 in grant funding from the
   California Department of Education for a school-based
   health center planning project. Worked with a team of
   stakeholders to develop a strong proposal that outlined the
   need for the health center and the anticipated outcomes for
   students and the community. Conducted research on
   similar programs and assessed the feasibility of the project.
3. *Grant Writing Training Workshops - Developed and led*
   grant writing training workshops for local non-profit
   organizations and community groups. Workshops covered
   topics such as grant research, proposal development,
   budgeting and financial management, and relationship
   building. Received positive feedback from workshop
   participants and successfully increased the capacity of
   these organizations to secure grant funding.
4. *Capacity Building Grant Proposal - Secured $175,000 in*
   grant funding from the California Wellness Foundation for
   a capacity building project for a local non-profit
   organization. Developed a comprehensive proposal that
   outlined the organization's goals, challenges, and
   strategies for building capacity. Conducted research on
   best practices for capacity building in non-profit
   organizations and worked with the organization's
   leadership to develop a realistic and feasible plan.

References:

Available upon request.

Finding Grant Writing Jobs: Strategies for Job Seekers

If you have the skills and experience necessary to become a grant writer, the next step is to find a job that matches your interests and qualifications. While grant writing jobs are available in various industries and organizations, finding one that fits your needs can be challenging.

In this article, we will discuss strategies for job seekers to find grant writing jobs.

1. **Research Job Postings:**

   Job search engines and websites are a great way to start your job search. Websites like Indeed, Glassdoor, and LinkedIn can help you find grant writing jobs in your area or any location. It is essential to research potential employers to determine if their mission aligns with your interests. Research the company culture and the type of grants they offer to determine if it is the right fit for you.

2. **Attend Networking Events:**

   Networking events offer a unique opportunity to meet other grant writers and professionals in the non-profit industry. Attend conferences, workshops, and networking events in your local area to network with other professionals and learn more about potential job opportunities.

3. **Reach Out to Non-Profits and Charities:**

   Many non-profit organizations and charities rely on grant writers to help them secure funding. Contacting these organizations directly can help you learn about grant writing opportunities that are not listed on job search websites. Consider reaching out to these organizations and inquire if they have any grant writing job openings.

4. **Use Social Media:**

Social media platforms like Twitter, Facebook, and LinkedIn can help you connect with other grant writers and non-profit organizations. Join groups and follow organizations that are of interest to you. This will keep you up to date on job opportunities and allow you to connect with potential employers.

5. Volunteer or Intern:

Volunteering or interning is an excellent way to gain experience in the non-profit industry and build relationships with potential employers. This type of work also provides opportunities for you to learn more about the organization and determine if it's a good fit for you.

6. Create an Online Portfolio:

An online portfolio is a collection of your best writing samples and your resume. This is a great way to showcase your writing skills and provide potential employers with examples of your work. You can create an online portfolio on a website or through a social media platform like LinkedIn.

7. Consider Freelance Work:

Freelance grant writing is another option for job seekers. Many non-profit organizations and charities hire freelance grant writers to help them secure funding. Freelance grant writing also provides you with the flexibility to work from home and set your own hours.

Here are some additional tips for finding grant writing jobs:

1. **Network**: Networking is a powerful tool when it comes to finding job opportunities. Attend industry events, join professional associations, and connect with other professionals in the field. This can help you learn about job openings and gain valuable insights from other grant writers.
2. **Look for job postings**: Search online job boards and professional associations for job postings. Many grant writing jobs are listed on websites like Indeed, SimplyHired, and LinkedIn. You can also check the websites of organizations that you are interested in working for to see if they have any job openings.
3. **Check with temp agencies**: Temp agencies can often help connect you with grant writing opportunities. They may have temporary or contract positions available that can help you build your experience.
4. **Consider freelancing**: Freelancing can be a great way to build your grant writing skills and gain experience. Look for opportunities to write grants for smaller organizations, such as local non-profits, to build your portfolio. Websites like Upwork and Freelancer can also connect you with grant writing opportunities.
5. **Contact grant writing firms**: Many organizations specialize in grant writing and offer their services to non-profits and other organizations. Reach out to these firms to see if they have any job opportunities available.
6. **Follow up**: If you have applied for a grant writing job and haven't heard back, follow up with the employer to express your continued interest in the position. This can show your dedication and interest in the role.

By using these strategies, you can increase your chances of finding grant writing jobs and building your career in the field.

Freelance grant writing: tips and strategies for success

As a freelance grant writer, you have the freedom to work on your own terms and take on projects that interest you. However, with this freedom comes the responsibility to manage your time, finances, and relationships with clients effectively.

Here are some tips and strategies to help you succeed as a freelance grant writer.

1. **Build your reputation**: As a freelance grant writer, your reputation is everything. Building a strong reputation takes time, but there are a few things you can do to speed up the process. First, deliver high-quality work that meets or exceeds your client's expectations. Second, communicate clearly and promptly with your clients. Third, be professional in all your dealings with clients, even if you encounter a difficult client or a difficult project.

2. **Set clear expectations:** One of the most important things you can do as a freelance grant writer is to set clear expectations with your clients. This includes setting expectations around project scope, timeline, and fees. It's important to have a written contract that outlines these details, so both you and your client are clear on what is expected.

3. **Manage your time effectively**: As a freelance grant writer, you'll likely be juggling multiple projects at once. To stay on top of everything, it's important to manage your time effectively. Use a calendar or project management tool to keep track of deadlines and project timelines. Prioritize your work based on the deadlines and complexity of each project.

4. **Stay organized**: Staying organized is key to success as a freelance grant writer. Keep track of your invoices, contracts, and other important documents. Use a project

management tool to keep all your project-related documents in one place. Keep your workspace clean and free of clutter, so you can focus on your work.

5. **Network with other grant writers**: Networking is an important part of any freelance career. Connect with other grant writers through professional organizations or social media. Attend industry events and conferences to meet other grant writers and potential clients. Networking can lead to new job opportunities and help you build a strong reputation in the industry.

6. **Continuously improve your skills**: As a freelance grant writer, it's important to continuously improve your skills. This can include taking courses or workshops to learn new skills, reading industry publications to stay up-to-date on trends and best practices, and working with a mentor to improve your writing and grant writing strategies. The more you invest in your skills, the more competitive you will be as a freelance grant writer.

7. **Manage your finances:** Managing your finances is an important part of freelance grant writing. Keep track of your income and expenses, and set aside money for taxes. Use invoicing software to send professional-looking invoices and track your payments. Consider working with a financial advisor or accountant to help you manage your finances and plan for the future.

Here are some additional tips and strategies for success as a freelance grant writer:

1. **Develop a strong portfolio:** As a freelance grant writer, your portfolio is a crucial tool for demonstrating your experience and expertise to potential clients. Make sure to include a variety of samples that showcase your writing style and ability to develop successful grant proposals.

2. **Network with other professionals**: Building relationships with other professionals in the nonprofit and fundraising industries can help you stay up-to-date on current trends and opportunities. Attend industry events, join professional organizations, and connect with other grant writers to expand your network.
3. **Focus on your strengths**: Determine what areas of grant writing you excel in, and focus your marketing efforts on those areas. This will help you stand out from other freelance grant writers and attract clients who need your specific skills and experience.
4. **Develop a niche**: Specializing in a particular area of grant writing, such as healthcare or education, can help you build a reputation as an expert in that field. This can lead to more opportunities and higher-paying clients.
5. **Set clear expectations with clients**: Before taking on a project, make sure to discuss the scope of the work, deadlines, and payment terms with your client. This can help prevent misunderstandings and ensure that you and your client are on the same page throughout the project.
6. **Stay organized**: Managing multiple clients and projects can be challenging as a freelance grant writer. Use tools such as project management software or a calendar to keep track of deadlines and ensure that you are meeting your clients' expectations.
7. **Continuously improve your skills**: Stay up-to-date on the latest trends and best practices in grant writing by attending workshops, webinars, and training sessions. This can help you stay competitive in the industry and attract higher-paying clients.

By following these tips and strategies, you can set yourself up for success as a freelance grant writer and build a successful career in the industry.

Developing a Marketing Strategy: Strategies for Building your Grant Writing

As a freelance grant writer, it's essential to have a solid marketing strategy to build your business and attract clients.

The following are some effective strategies that can help you market your grant writing services and increase your chances of success.

1. **Develop a website**: Having a website can make a significant impact on your business. It is a great way to showcase your experience, education, and skills to potential clients. A website can also help you establish credibility and build trust with clients. Ensure that your website is easy to navigate and contains essential information about your services, rates, and contact details.
2. **Create a portfolio of your work:** A portfolio can demonstrate your experience and writing skills. You can showcase your previous grant proposals, letters of inquiry, and evaluations in your portfolio. Creating a portfolio can also help you identify your strengths and areas for improvement.
3. **Utilize social media**: Social media platforms such as LinkedIn, Twitter, and Facebook can be used to promote your grant writing services. You can use social media to share information about your work, promote your website, and connect with potential clients.
4. **Attend networking events**: Attending networking events can help you connect with potential clients. You can also gain knowledge about the latest trends and changes in the industry. Try to attend events such as grant writing workshops, nonprofit conferences, and professional networking events.
5. **Utilize online marketplaces**: Online marketplaces like Upwork, Freelancer, and Fiverr can be an excellent way to

find grant writing jobs. These websites allow clients to post job listings, and freelancers can bid on them. You can create a profile on these websites and bid on grant writing jobs that match your skills and experience.

6. **Leverage your network**: Networking can be one of the most effective ways to promote your business. Let your friends, family, and colleagues know that you offer grant writing services. They may have connections that could lead to potential clients.

7. **Create a marketing plan**: Creating a marketing plan can help you identify your target audience, marketing channels, and budget. A marketing plan can help you focus your efforts and resources on activities that are most likely to generate new business.

Part 6

Professional Development In Grant writing

Professional development is an essential part of any career, and grant writing is no exception. Whether you are a beginner or a seasoned grant writer, there are always new skills to learn and ways to improve.

In this section, we will explore some strategies for professional development in grant writing.

1. **Attend conferences and workshops**: Attending conferences and workshops is a great way to learn about the latest trends and best practices in grant writing. It also provides an opportunity to network with other professionals in the field. Look for local, regional, and national conferences and workshops that offer sessions specifically geared towards grant writing.
2. **Join professional organizations:** Joining a professional organization can provide access to a wealth of resources and networking opportunities. Organizations such as the Grant Professionals Association (GPA) and the American Grant Writers' Association (AGWA) offer resources such as job listings, webinars, and certification programs.
3. **Take online courses**: There are many online courses and certificate programs available that can help you improve your grant writing skills. These courses cover topics such as grant proposal writing, budgeting, and project management. They can be completed at your own pace and are often more affordable than traditional in-person courses.
4. **Seek out mentors**: Mentors can be a valuable resource for professional development. Look for experienced grant

writers in your field and ask if they would be willing to mentor you. A mentor can offer guidance, feedback, and advice on how to improve your skills.

5. **Read industry publications**: Staying up-to-date with the latest news and trends in the grant writing industry is crucial for professional development. Reading industry publications such as GrantStation Insider, Philanthropy News Digest, and The Chronicle of Philanthropy can provide valuable insights into the latest grant writing strategies and funding opportunities.

6. **Volunteer**: Volunteering for a non-profit organization or serving on a grant review panel can provide hands-on experience with the grant writing process. This can help you gain a better understanding of what funders are looking for in a grant proposal and can help you improve your own grant writing skills.

7. **Attend webinars**: Webinars are a convenient way to learn about specific topics related to grant writing. Many organizations offer free webinars that cover topics such as writing successful grant proposals, budgeting, and program evaluation.

8. **Pursue professional certification**: Professional certification can help demonstrate your expertise in grant writing to potential clients and employers. The Grant Professional Certification (GPC) offered by the Grant Professionals Certification Institute (GPCI) is a widely recognized certification for grant writing professionals.

Professional development: Strategies for Continuing Education and growth

Professional development is essential in any field, including grant writing. As a grant writer, staying up to date with the latest trends and best practices can help you to become a more successful grant writer and expand your career opportunities.

In this section, we will discuss some strategies for continuing education and growth in grant writing.

1. Attend Workshops and Conferences

Attending workshops and conferences is an excellent way to learn new skills, gain new insights, and network with other professionals in the field. There are numerous workshops and conferences offered both in-person and online, so finding one that fits your needs and schedule should not be difficult.

When choosing a workshop or conference to attend, consider the topic, the speaker, and the location. Make sure that the workshop or conference aligns with your professional goals, and that the speaker is well-respected in the field. Attending a conference in a desirable location can also be an excellent opportunity to explore new places and make new connections.

2. Pursue Professional Certifications

Pursuing a professional certification in grant writing can demonstrate to potential clients or employers that you are committed to the field and have a solid understanding of best practices. Some examples of professional certifications in grant writing include the Grant Professional Certification (GPC) from the Grant Professionals Certification Institute, and the Certified Fund Raising Executive (CFRE) from the Association of Fundraising Professionals.

To obtain a professional certification, you will need to meet specific requirements, such as a certain number of years of experience in the field and passing an exam. Pursuing a professional certification can be a significant investment of time and money, but it can pay off in the long run with increased job opportunities and higher pay.

3. Read Industry Publications

Staying up to date with the latest trends and best practices in the grant writing industry is essential for professional development. One way to do this is by reading industry publications such as Grant Station Insider, The Chronicle of Philanthropy, and Nonprofit Quarterly.

These publications cover a wide range of topics, including fundraising strategies, grant writing tips, and new grant opportunities. Reading industry publications can help you to stay informed about changes in the field and keep your skills current.

4. Network with Other Professionals

Networking with other professionals in the field can help you to learn new skills, gain new insights, and discover new job opportunities. Joining a professional organization such as the Grant Professionals Association or the Association of Fundraising Professionals can be an excellent way to meet other professionals in the field and attend networking events.

Attending networking events can also help you to build relationships with other professionals in the field and learn about new job opportunities. Networking is a critical component of professional development and can lead to new opportunities for growth and career advancement.

5. Participate in Online Communities

Participating in online communities can be an excellent way to connect with other professionals in the grant writing field and learn new skills. Social media platforms such as LinkedIn and Twitter can be a great way to connect with other professionals and stay up to date with the latest trends and best practices.

Joining online communities such as grant writing forums or Facebook groups can also be an excellent way to connect with other professionals in the field and learn new skills. Participating in online communities can be an effective way to stay engaged in the field and keep your skills current.

Overcoming Rejection: Coping with the Challenges of Grant Writing

Grant writing can be a challenging and competitive field, and unfortunately, rejection is a common occurrence. While it can be disheartening to receive a rejection letter, it's important to remember that it doesn't necessarily mean your proposal wasn't strong or your writing wasn't good.

Rejection is often a result of factors outside of your control, such as the funder's priorities, available funds, or the competitiveness of the applicant pool.

That said, rejection can still be difficult to deal with.

Here are some strategies for coping with rejection and using it to grow and improve as a grant writer.

1. **Allow yourself to feel disappointment**: It's natural to feel disappointed or even upset when you receive a rejection letter. Acknowledge your feelings and give yourself

permission to feel disappointed. It's okay to take a break, do something nice for yourself, or talk to a trusted friend or mentor about your feelings.

2. **Review the feedback**: Many funders will offer feedback on your proposal, even if it was rejected. Take advantage of this feedback and carefully review it. Try to approach the feedback with an open mind and a willingness to learn from it. Look for patterns in the feedback that may point to areas for improvement in your writing or proposal development process.

3. **Reflect on what you learned**: Rejection can be a learning opportunity. Think about what you learned from the process of writing and submitting the proposal, and from the feedback you received. Were there areas where you felt less confident or areas where you struggled? What could you have done differently? Use this information to make changes and improvements in your future work.

4. **Keep a growth mindset**: Remember that rejection is not a reflection of your worth or talent as a grant writer. It's simply a part of the process. Instead of dwelling on the rejection, focus on what you can do to improve and grow as a writer. Try to cultivate a growth mindset, which means believing that your abilities can be developed through hard work, dedication, and learning.

5. **Take action**: After reflecting on the feedback and your experience, take action to improve your writing or proposal development process. This might include seeking out additional training or education, reaching out to a mentor or peer for advice, or practicing your writing and editing skills.

6. **Keep going**: Remember that rejection is a normal part of the grant writing process. It's important to keep going and continue submitting proposals, even if you receive rejections along the way. The more you write and submit, the more you will learn and grow as a grant writer.

Networking and Community Building: Strategies for Connecting with other Grant Writers

Grant writing can be a rewarding but challenging profession. As a grant writer, it is essential to have a support network and community of fellow professionals who understand the unique demands of the job. Networking and community building are key strategies for connecting with other grant writers, sharing experiences, and gaining insights into the profession.

Here are some strategies for building your network and community as a grant writer:

1. **Join Professional Associations**: One of the easiest ways to build your network and connect with other grant writers is by joining a professional association. There are several national and regional associations for grant writers, such as the Grant Professionals Association (GPA), National Grant Management Association (NGMA), and the Association of Fundraising Professionals (AFP). These organizations provide a platform to connect with other professionals, access to training and educational resources, and opportunities to attend conferences and events.
2. **Attend Conferences and Workshops**: Attending conferences and workshops is another effective way to connect with other grant writers. These events provide an opportunity to meet other professionals, learn from experts in the field, and gain new skills and knowledge. Attending conferences and workshops can also help you stay up-to-date on the latest trends and best practices in the industry.
3. **Participate in Online Communities**: The internet has made it easier than ever to connect with other grant writers online. There are several online communities, such as LinkedIn groups, Facebook groups, and Twitter chats,

where grant writers can connect, share experiences, and learn from each other. These online communities provide a convenient way to build your network and connect with professionals from around the world.

4. **Volunteer and Internship Opportunities**: Another way to connect with other grant writers is by volunteering or taking on an internship. Volunteering can provide you with opportunities to work with other professionals, gain practical experience, and build your skills. Many nonprofit organizations and community groups are often looking for grant writers to assist them with their proposals. Taking on an internship can also provide you with valuable experience, and you can use the opportunity to network and connect with other professionals.

5. **Collaborate with Other Grant Writers**: Collaborating with other grant writers is an effective way to build your network and community. You can work together on a project, share resources, and learn from each other. Collaborating with other professionals can also help you build your portfolio, gain new skills, and enhance your reputation in the field.

Part 7
Conclusion

Grant writing can be a challenging but rewarding career path. Whether you are just starting out or have been in the industry for years, there are always new strategies and best practices to learn and implement. In this guide, we have covered a wide range of topics to help you succeed as a grant writer, from the basics of grant writing to developing a marketing strategy for your business.

One of the most important things to keep in mind as a grant writer is the need to stay organized and on top of deadlines. This means having a clear understanding of the requirements for each grant proposal, as well as a system in place for keeping track of deadlines and other key information. It can also be helpful to use project management tools or other software to stay organized and manage your workload.

Another crucial aspect of successful grant writing is effective communication. This includes not only writing skills, but also the ability to build relationships with funders and collaborate with partners. By focusing on building strong relationships and using clear, compelling language, you can increase your chances of success and stand out in a crowded field.

Professional development is also essential for grant writers who want to stay at the top of their game. This can include everything from attending conferences and workshops to taking online courses and reading industry publications. By continuing to learn and grow, you can stay up to date on the latest trends and best practices in grant writing, and ensure that your skills are always in demand.

Finally, it's important to remember that rejection is a normal part of the grant writing process. Even the most experienced grant writers face rejection from time to time. The key is to stay positive and keep working on your skills and relationships. With perseverance, a willingness to learn, and a commitment to excellence, you can build a successful career as a grant writer and make a real difference in the world.

Future of Grant Writing

Grant writing has been a crucial element in the nonprofit sector for a long time. As the nonprofit industry evolves, so does grant writing. In this article, we'll explore the future of grant writing and how the industry will continue to change.

Technology advancements will play a significant role in the future of grant writing. The use of grant writing software and online platforms will become even more widespread. These tools help to streamline the grant writing process, allowing grant writers to save time, stay organized, and work more efficiently. Technology will continue to evolve, and we can expect to see more advanced grant writing software and tools that cater to the specific needs of grant writers.

Another trend we can expect to see in the future is the use of data and analytics in grant writing. More and more organizations are using data to drive decision-making, and grant writing will not be an exception.

Grant writers will need to have a good understanding of data analysis and be able to integrate it into their proposals effectively. This means that grant writers will have to learn how to collect and analyze data, which will require them to acquire new skills and knowledge.

Grant writers will also need to be proficient in writing proposals that resonate with funders. This means that grant writers will need to have a deep understanding of the funding organizations and their goals. They will need to be able to develop proposals that align with the mission and values of the funding organizations. The ability to communicate effectively with funders and build relationships will be more important than ever before.

In the future, grant writing will become more competitive, with more organizations seeking funding. As a result, grant writers will need to be creative in their proposals and differentiate themselves from other organizations. Grant writers will need to think outside the box and develop proposals that are unique and innovative. They will need to show that their organization is capable of delivering results that go beyond the expected outcomes.

Grant writers will also need to be proficient in evaluating the impact of their proposals. This means that grant writers will need to be able to measure the outcomes of the programs they propose accurately. They will need to be able to collect data, analyze it, and report on the results of their proposals. Grant writers will have to work with program managers and data analysts to develop effective evaluation plans that can measure the impact of the programs they propose.

The future of grant writing is exciting and challenging. Grant writers will need to adapt to new trends, develop new skills and knowledge, and stay up-to-date with the latest technology and best practices. The nonprofit industry will continue to grow, and grant writing will be a critical component in securing funding for these organizations.

Final thoughts and advice for aspiring grant
Grant writing can be a fulfilling and lucrative career for those who have a passion for making a difference in the world. However, it can also be a challenging and competitive field to break into. As you begin your journey as an aspiring grant writer, there are a few final thoughts and pieces of advice that can help you succeed and thrive in this industry.

First and foremost, it's important to remember that grant writing is not just about writing; it's about making a real impact on people's lives. As a grant writer, you have the opportunity to connect with funders and help them see the value and potential impact of the programs and initiatives that you are advocating for. This means that you need to be passionate and committed to the causes you are writing for. It's not just about earning a paycheck; it's about making a positive difference in the world.

Secondly, it's essential to stay up-to-date with the latest trends and best practices in grant writing. The field of grant writing is constantly evolving, and funders are always looking for new and innovative ways to create positive change. By staying current with the latest research and industry news, you can position yourself as a thought leader in the field and offer valuable insights and expertise to your clients.

Networking and building relationships with other grant writers can also be instrumental in your success. Joining professional organizations, attending industry events and conferences, and participating in online forums and social media groups can help you connect with other professionals in the field, learn about new opportunities, and gain valuable insights and advice.

Maintain a positive attitude and perseverance in the face of rejection and setbacks. The grant writing process can be long and arduous, and it's not uncommon to experience rejection or face difficult challenges along the way. However, it's important to remain resilient, learn from your experiences, and keep pushing forward. As the old adage goes, "Rome wasn't built in a day," and the same is true for grant writing. Success in this field often requires patience, persistence, and a willingness to learn and grow from your experiences.

In conclusion, grant writing is an exciting and rewarding career that requires a unique combination of skills, passion, and dedication. By following the strategies and advice outlined in this guide, you can position yourself for success and make a positive difference in the world through your work as a grant writer. Good luck on your journey, and remember to stay passionate, persistent, and always willing to learn and grow!

CONTACT
EMAIL: grantwritingacademy@gmail.com
Website: grantwritingacad.org

About The Book

Introducing "Breaking Into Grant Writing" - the ultimate guide to jumpstart your career as a successful grant writer! This comprehensive book is written by an experienced grant writer, covering everything you need to know about the grant writing process.

With engaging and informative writing, this book will take you on a journey through the world of grant writing, offering practical tips, expert advice, and real-life examples. From researching funding opportunities to crafting winning proposals, you will learn the tools and techniques to write successful grant proposals.

Whether you're a beginner looking to enter the grant writing field, or a seasoned writer seeking to enhance your skills, this book is the perfect resource. It covers all aspects of grant writing, including developing effective cover letters, creating impactful data and evaluation plans, building a portfolio, finding grant writing jobs, and much more.

With this book, you'll gain the confidence and knowledge to excel in the grant writing industry. The practical examples and step-by-step guidance make it easy to understand the grant writing process and put your skills to work.

Don't let the lack of knowledge hold you back from pursuing your passion for grant writing. Get your copy of "Breaking Into Grant Writing" and start your journey to becoming a successful grant writer today!

About the Author

Queen Israel is a highly experienced and accomplished grant writing consultant with over 10 years of experience in the field.

With a passion for helping organizations achieve their goals through grant funding, she has dedicated her career to assisting nonprofit organizations in securing the funding they need to make a real impact in their communities.

She has worked with numerous organizations in a variety of industries, including healthcare, education, environmental conservation, and social justice, among others.

Throughout her career, Queen has earned a reputation for her exceptional writing skills, strategic thinking, and collaborative approach.

When she is not busy helping organizations secure grant funding, Queen enjoys spending time with her family and exploring the great outdoors. She currently lives in Nigeria with her husband and son.